D1600782

Lost and Buried Treasures of the Civil War

Lost and Buried Treasures of the Civil War

W. C. Jameson

LYONS
PRESS

Guilford, Connecticut

An imprint of The Rowman & Littlefield Publishing Group, Inc.
4501 Forbes Blvd., Ste. 200
Lanham, MD 20706
www.rowman.com

Distributed by NATIONAL BOOK NETWORK

British Library Cataloguing in Publication Information available

Library of Congress Cataloging-in-Publication Data

Names: Jameson, W. C., 1942- author.
Title: Lost and buried treasures of the Civil War / W.C. Jameson.
Description: Guilford, Connecticut : Lyons Press, [2019] | Includes index.
Identifiers: LCCN 2018054261 (print) | LCCN 2018060778 (ebook) | ISBN 9781493040766 (e-book) | ISBN 9781493040759 (hardcover : alk. paper)
Subjects: LCSH: United States—History—Civil War, 1861-1865—Antiquities. | Treasure troves—United States. | Treasure troves—Southern States. | Treasure troves—Northeastern States.
Classification: LCC E646.5 (ebook) | LCC E646.5 .J36 2019 (print) | DDC 973.7/6—dc23
LC record available at https://lccn.loc.gov/2018054261

Printed in the United States of America

Contents

Introduction vii

CHAPTER 1: Corporal Henry Fletcher's Lost Blue
Quartz Gold. 1
CHAPTER 2: Rebel Coin Cache in Cobb County, Georgia 5
CHAPTER 3: The Lost Treasure of Colonel Norman Frisby 11
CHAPTER 4: The Lost Parlange Fortune. 17
CHAPTER 5: Sunken Confederate Treasure and Arms off the
South Carolina Coast 22
CHAPTER 6: The Treasure in the Well 26
CHAPTER 7: Lost Yankee Payroll .31
CHAPTER 8: Kegs of Gold and Silver Coins. 36
CHAPTER 9: Lost Confederate Payroll. 40
CHAPTER 10: The Lipscomb Plantation Treasure 44
CHAPTER 11: Buried Weapons at Cross Hollows, Arkansas 48
CHAPTER 12: Callahan Mountain Treasure 51
CHAPTER 13: The Alonzus Hall Treasure 53
CHAPTER 14: Lost Cherokee Gold 58
CHAPTER 15: The Incredible Journey of the Confederate
Treasury 62
CHAPTER 16: The Lost Treasures of General John H. Morgan 70
CHAPTER 17: Field of Gold and Silver Coins 76
CHAPTER 18: Buried Union Army Payroll. 81
CHAPTER 19: The Bechtler Coins .84
CHAPTER 20: Pots of Gold 90
CHAPTER 21: The Lost Gold of Cohutta Mountain. 95
CHAPTER 22: Civil War Outlaw Treasure Cave 100

Chapter 23: John Crismo's Lost Treasure 106
Chapter 24: Poor Valley Treasure 110
Chapter 25: The Lost Treasure of the Gray Ghost. 114
Chapter 26: Buckhannon River Valley Treasure 118
Chapter 27: Abandoned Union Payroll 123
Chapter 28: Confederate Treasure in North Carolina 125
Chapter 29: Sunken Civil War Firearms. 130
Chapter 30: Confederate Silver Cache in Pennsylvania 134
Chapter 31: Lost Confederate Treasure Cache in Vermont 141

Index 149
About the Author 155

INTRODUCTION

WITH THE POSSIBLE EXCEPTION OF THE GREAT GOLD RUSH TO CALIfornia and other western parts of the country during the mid-nineteenth century, it has been estimated that more treasure in the form of gold and silver coins and ingots, as well as jewelry and other family valuables, were lost and buried during, and as a result of, the Civil War.

During this historic era in the growing United States, banks were far less stable than they are now, and many individuals who possessed any kind of wealth often hid it close to home. We know that several stored their fortunes and valuables in closets or beneath floorboards. More than a few buried their savings in one or more locations on their property or nearby. As the war raged on, lives were disrupted and many were forced to flee their land, never to return to retrieve their riches. Some were slain, and the knowledge of their valuables caches was lost. Most of these fortunes and treasures remain unrecovered to this day.

In addition, the militaries of both Union and Confederate forces were known to transport a great deal of wealth in the form of coins and other valuable specie. Much of this was oriented toward payroll shipments to the soldiers in the field. Many more millions were en route to purchase arms and ammunition when they were lost, stolen, or otherwise hidden. Other fortunes were misplaced or cached due to circumstances of the War between the States.

With the advent of renewed interest in lost mines and buried treasures of the Civil War, along with the availability of state-of-the-art metal detection devices, a number of professional and amateur fortune hunters have undertaken to locate and recover many millions of dollars' worth of gold, silver, and other valuable items. A few of these treasures have been recovered, but the vast majority remain lost.

① Corporal Henry Fletcher's Lost Blue Quartz Gold
② Confederate Coin Cache in Cobb County, Georgia
③ The Lost Treasure of Colonel Norman Frisby
④ The Lost Parlange Fortune
⑤ Sunken Confederate Treasure and Arms off the South Carolina Coast
⑥ The Treasure in the Well
⑦ Lost Yankee Payroll
⑧ Kegs of Gold and Silver Coins
⑨ Lost Confederate Payroll
⑩ The Lipscomb Plantation Treasure
⑪ Buried Weapons at Cross Hollows, Arkansas
⑫ Callahan Mountain Treasure
⑬ The Alonzus Hall Treasure
⑭ Lost Cherokee Gold
⑮ The Incredible Journey of the Confederate Treasury
⑯ The Lost Treasure of General John H. Morgan
⑰ Field of Gold and Silver Coins
⑱ Buried Union Army Payroll
⑲ The Bechtler Coins
⑳ Pots of Gold
㉑ The Lost Gold of Cohutta Mountain
㉒ Civil War Outlaw Treasure Cave
㉓ John Crismo's Lost Treasure
㉔ Poor Valley Treasure
㉕ The Lost Treasure of the Gray Ghost
㉖ Buckhannon River Valley Treasure
㉗ Abandoned Union Payroll
㉘ Confederate Treasure in North Carolina
㉙ Sunken Civil War Firearms
㉚ Confederate Silver Cache in Pennsylvania
㉛ Lost Confederate Treasure Cache in Vermont

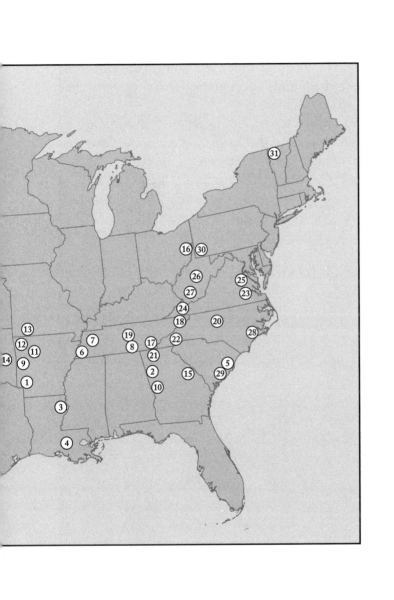

To a professional treasure hunter, the era of the Civil War is attractive in a number of ways. Many of the lost or cached military payrolls are documented, so the fortune at the end of the search remains a real one as opposed to a folkloric or mythical one. The truth is, there are millions of dollars' worth of such payrolls waiting to be discovered. Further, recovered artifacts associated with both the Union and Confederate armies can sometimes yield impressively high values among collectors. Recovered weapons caches find a viable market.

Most tales of lost mines and buried treasures are steeped in history and/or lore. The added element of the fascinating era of the Civil War adds a particular level of interest and excitement to the quest.

For the first time, an exhaustively researched collection of some of the most notable and exciting lost treasures of the Civil War is presented in the following pages.

CHAPTER ONE

Corporal Henry Fletcher's Lost Blue Quartz Gold

THE GENTLE ROLLING HILLS AND VALLEYS OF ARKANSAS'S OUACHITA Mountains provided few obstacles to the mounted company of Confederate cavalry as it picked its way along a seldom used trail. The soldiers were on their way to the tiny community of Sugar Grove located several miles to the east of their current position. There, the company would rendezvous with another that awaited them in camp. Single file, the horsemen wound along the bottom of Brushy Creek Valley paralleling the small, sinuous stream. The narrow valley was bordered by low, folded sandstone ridges characteristic of this range.

Here and there along the slopes of the mountains the sandstone had eroded away, exposing outcrops of granite, providing evidence that much of the range was underlain by this intrusive rock.

The valley supported a few farmers who grazed cattle and horses on the modest meadows that extended out along both sides of the creek. The forested hillsides showed evidence of timber cutting, and in the distance a sawmill could be seen.

The lieutenant leading the command ordered a brief halt so horses and men could water at the creek. During the stop, one of the cavalrymen, Corporal Henry Fletcher, complained of stomach cramps and requested permission to lie in the shade of a nearby tree. Several minutes later, the lieutenant ordered the company back onto the trail. Fletcher asked for more time to rest in hopes of easing his discomfort. The officer agreed and instructed him to catch up when he could.

Fletcher unsaddled his mount and staked it on a patch of grass near the tree. Not far away, he spotted a shady recess in an adjacent hillside. Next to it, a dripping spring issued from the rock. The soldier walked over to the shallow cave, hoping to find a comfortable place to nap for a short time before rejoining his company.

On arriving, Fletcher stepped over to the tiny spring seeping out of the rock three feet from the ground. The clear water was cool and issued from a crack in the sandstone, trickling down the rock in a thin, cascading waterfall. A small pool sixteen inches in diameter had formed on the cave floor. From this, the overflow trickled over one edge and down the gentle slope before seeping into the soft earth five feet away.

Fletcher was bending toward the dripping water to drink when he spotted a glint of color a few feet away. A thin outcrop of granite protruded from the sedimentary rock, and down the middle of the exposed intrusion was a vein of quartz of a striking blue. After slaking his thirst, Fletcher, intrigued by the strange quartz, hammered several chunks from the vein using the butt of his handgun. Examining it closely, he spotted a dense web of some kind of mineral embedded within. He placed the pieces in his knapsack and settled down for a short nap.

Fletcher awoke one hour later. Feeling much better, he walked over to his horse, saddled it, and rode away to rejoin his companions. He told none of them about his discovery of the blue quartz.

Several weeks passed, and Fletcher's cavalry company was camped just beyond Fort Smith, Arkansas. When the soldier was granted some time off, he rode into town and showed the blue quartz to a man known to have some mining experience. After examining the rock closely, he informed Fletcher that he had never seen quartz of that particular shade of blue and suggested that it might be rare. Even more interesting, he told the cavalryman, the quartz contained threads of a very high grade of gold ore. He explained that if it could be mined in sufficient quantity, it would yield a fortune.

Because of his commitment to the Confederate army, Fletcher had no opportunity to revisit the shallow cave in Brushy Creek Valley and the gold-filled vein of blue quartz. He decided he would remain patient. When the time came for him to be released from his military obligation, he planned to return to the location and mine the fortune in gold ore that awaited him there.

Time passed. Within days of receiving his discharge, Fletcher traveled to Fort Smith and outfitted himself with some mining tools, two mules, and enough provisions to last a few weeks. He returned to the Brushy Creek Valley in search of the exposed granite and the vein of blue quartz. At night, sitting by his campfire, Fletcher dreamed of the wealth he would soon possess and the life of ease and luxury it would provide.

Shortly after arriving in the valley, however, Fletcher became confused. He had difficulty recognizing any pertinent landmarks, and a recent flood had changed the appearance of the valley floor. Furthermore, additional timbering by the region's residents had laid bare portions of the hillsides, exposing the topsoil to erosion from heavy runoff following severe rains. Tons of this topsoil was removed from the slopes and deposited into the valley below. Disoriented, Fletcher nevertheless pursued his search for the gold. Three and a half weeks of searching yielded nothing, and Fletcher's provisions began running low. He returned to Fort Smith to resupply.

This experience was to be repeated often. Years passed, and Henry Fletcher returned to Brushy Creek Valley many times in search of the ever-elusive gold in the vein of mysterious blue quartz. Each expedition met with failure. By now, the tale of Fletcher's lost vein of gold-filled quartz was widely known throughout portions of Arkansas's Ouachita Mountains, and the hopeful former Confederate soldier would occasionally meet other gold seekers prospecting the valley.

Years of constant exposure to the natural elements caused Fletcher's health to deteriorate. Seized with a severe bout of pneumonia, he was hospitalized in Fort Smith, where he was kept for weeks. Following his discharge from the hospital, Fletcher remained in the town, trying to recuperate so he could continue his quest for the gold. It was not to happen. Several months after being treated, Henry Fletcher died. To the end, he continued to insist that his story of the discovery of gold in Brushy Creek Valley was true.

A few years following the death of Henry Fletcher, it was announced that gold was discovered at Redman's Mill, a small community located in Brushy Creek Valley a short distance from where Fletcher is believed to have located the gold-filled blue quartz vein.

During the 1990s, a farmer who lived in Brushy Creek Valley revealed that he was well acquainted with the tale of the lost gold and had spoken with several men who still came to the region to search for Henry Fletcher's vein of ore. He also claimed to know where the shallow cave with the spring was located. During an interview, the farmer stated that, although he had dug small amounts of gold from the quartz vein from time to time, there was not enough of the ore to warrant a full-scale mining operation. He suggested that such a thing would be disruptive to his neighbors and the peaceful environment that existed there. He reminded the interviewer that that was exactly what had happened during the mining of gold at Redman's Mill in the 1880s. The farmer refused to show the location of the gold to anyone. Two months following the interview, he passed away.

Henry Fletcher spent most of his adult life trying to relocate the gold he found when a young man. With the passage of years, many others have invested considerable time, energy, and resources into the same quest. Recent geological investigations undertaken in this part of the Ouachita Mountains has provided reason for excitement among contemporary prospectors and treasure hunters. As a result, more and more are arriving in Brushy Creek Valley and environs in search of gold.

With luck and patience, it is possible that a member of the current generation of gold seekers may happen upon Corporal Henry Fletcher's lost vein of gold-filled blue quartz.

Chapter Two

Rebel Coin Cache in Cobb County, Georgia

During the first months of 1864, the conflict and horror of the Civil War were gaining a frightening momentum. Northern and Southern soldiers and citizens alike were swept up in the fire and fury that appeared to have no end. Amassed Union forces began making significant inroads into the South, and residents grew fearful for their lives, property, and fortunes. As the Yankees encroached into the realm of the South, they slew all who stood in their way, stole or killed livestock, and burned towns to the ground. Invariably, they ransacked Southern banks and business institutions and confiscated all monetary assets.

A great percentage of Southerners were distrustful of banks long before the advent of the war. As they learned of the Union propensity for raiding such institutions, more and more of them removed their money and relocated it in some secret or obscure location in the ground on their property. It is believed that millions of dollars' worth of gold bullion, along with gold and silver coins and currency, jewelry, and other family valuables were hidden in this manner. Most of it, it is estimated, remains hidden to this day.

Union soldiers were aware of this practice and often invested significant time and energy into excavating large portions of the property surrounding Southern mansions and other residences.

An Atlanta, Georgia, businessman whose name has been lost to history learned of a force of approaching Yankee soldiers. Soon, he realized, the city would be under siege. Knowing his fortune in gold coins was in jeopardy, the businessman packed just over $100,000 worth into several heavy leather pouches. Enlisting the help of two slaves, he loaded the fortune onto a Western and Atlantic passenger train that was idling at the downtown Atlanta terminal in preparation for departure. Approaching the conductor, the businessman made arrangements to have his cargo, slaves, and himself dropped off at a remote location fifteen miles to the northwest of the train station and just across the Chattahoochee River in Cobb County. A gold coin passed from the hand of the businessman to the railroad employee.

An hour later, and after crossing the Chattahoochee River bridge, the train ground to a halt. Laboriously, the businessman and the two slaves unloaded the sacks of gold coins, placing them next to the railroad tracks. This done, a signal was given to the engineer and the train started forward. Moments later, after the train had disappeared around a bend in the distance, the businessman and the slaves hefted two sacks each and struck out on a seldom used trail that led into the woods toward the northeast.

The businessman, soft, weak, and overweight from decades of sitting behind a desk, had difficulty transporting the heavy sacks and was forced to stop often to rest. After traveling three hundred yards, the three men came to a large tree. Withdrawing a knife from his coat, the businessman slashed a long blaze chest high on the trunk. From this point, he proceeded three hundred yards to the north, followed by the slaves. On arriving at a large oak tree, he carved a deep "M" and "X" into the bole. Not far from the tree, he noted, was a freshwater spring that led to the Chattahoochee River.

Stepping off several paces from this spot, the businessman encountered a deep hole that had been formed when the large tree occupying the site had toppled over as a result of a previous storm. After having his slaves deposit the sacks of gold coins into the hole, the businessman led them back to the point near the railroad tracks, where they retrieved more pouches. In all, several trips were necessary to transport the gold coins to the cache site. Once all the sacks were placed into the hole, it was filled and covered with branches, leaves, and other debris to look much like the surrounding forest floor.

As a result of the effort of carrying the sacks and filling the holes, the businessman was forced to pause several times to catch his breath. His breathing was heavy and labored, and at times he placed a hand over his heart as if trying to control its rapid beating. During one of several rest stops, the businessman seated himself against the bole of the large oak tree, withdrew a piece of paper and a graphite from a coat pocket, and sketched a map showing the locations of the river, the railroad track, the marked trees, and the cache of gold coins. Several minutes later, he rose and led the slaves on the long trek back to Atlanta.

The businessman and the slaves were spotted as they passed the train station and made their way toward the center of town. It was the last anyone ever saw of the two workers. When asked later, the businessman claimed they ran away during the night. Years later, however, some voiced the opinion that, since the two men knew the secret location of the gold cache, the businessman had killed them.

It was the businessman's plan to return to the buried coin cache and retrieve his fortune when the war was over, but that did not happen. The effort of transporting and burying the heavy sacks of gold coins, along with the long and difficult hike from the cache site back to Atlanta, placed too great a strain on the already frail man. A few days after returning to his home, he suffered a heart attack and died.

While making arrangements for the funeral, the businessman's widow discovered the crudely drawn map along with some cryptic notes relating to the treasure cache. A plethora of family and business-related problems occupied her activities for several months, but when affairs were finally in order, she began formulating plans to travel the short distance to Cobb County and retrieve the fortune in gold coins buried by her late husband. On the week she planned to undertake the effort, however, General Sherman and his forces marched into Atlanta and destroyed the city. The widow decided to wait until hostilities ended before resuming her search for the buried treasure.

When the war finally came to an end, the widow renewed her plans to try to find the buried gold. For days she attempted to follow the directions she interpreted from the map, but between the inadequately represented information and her poor sense of direction and distance, she accomplished little more than getting lost in the forest. Distrustful of others when it came to the great wealth, she refused to allow anyone else to look at the map or accompany her on her searches. Anyone, that is, save for one exception, a railroad conductor.

During her searches, the widow always set out from the depot. Sometimes she encountered the conductor of the Western and Atlantic Railroad, and the two became friends. On one occasion, she asked him to pinpoint the exact location at which her husband and the two slaves left the train. On more than one occasion, the widow showed the conductor the crudely sketched map. Each time, he would commit as much of it as possible to memory. Later, he reproduced it for himself.

After several attempts at finding the treasure over a period of three and a half months, the widow abandoned her search and moved to Texas to live with relatives. Within days of her leaving town, the conductor took up the search for the gold. Like the widow, he had difficulty interpreting the map, and he found himself lost in the woods time after time. His searches for the treasure were often interrupted by the demands of his job with the railroad, so the conductor eventually resigned in order to devote all his energies to locating what he now referred to as the Lost Cobb County Coin Cache.

The conductor had no better luck than the widow, and he began to doubt that he had accurately interpreted the information from the original map. By his estimate, the conductor made over one hundred trips into the woods adjacent to the W&A Railroad tracks in search of the treasure of gold coins, all fruitless. After years of searching, he gave up.

Decades later, the conductor, now an old man, related the tale of the lost gold cache to a young man named John Maynard. The conductor had known Maynard when they both worked for the railroad. Excited and intrigued by the story of more than $100,000 worth of gold coins buried a short distance from the railroad tracks, Maynard decided he would look for it. He traveled to Texas, where he arranged a meeting with the businessman's widow, who was now quite aged. During their discussions, Maynard convinced her to give him the original map. He promised her that, should he be successful in recovering the gold, he would divide it evenly with her. The widow agreed to the proposition and sent Maynard away with the map and her blessing. On returning to Atlanta, Maynard resigned his job and spent the rest of his life searching for the gold. He never found it.

Many years later, when Maynard was elderly, he related the details of his search for the so-called Lost Cobb County Gold Cache to a young friend he had known for several years named H. L. Denman. One source has Denman working as a fireman on the Nashville, Chattanooga, and St. Louis Railroad; another stated he had been employed by the Western and Atlantic Railway from 1907 through 1950. At first, Denman considered the tale a combination of local folklore and the ramblings of an aged citizen, a tale that held no interest for him whatsoever. One day in 1907, however, Maynard located, and then showed Denman, the original treasure map he had obtained from the businessman's widow. Still, the curious fireman remained skeptical.

Over the course of the following months, Denman raised the subject of the lost treasure to other friends, many of whom were familiar with the tale. After listening to their versions of the story, often accompanied by reasonable opinions and observations, Denman grew convinced that the treasure did, indeed, exist. Following a return to Atlanta from an assignment on a train run, Denman decided to borrow the map from Maynard and make an attempt at locating the treasure himself. On arriving at Maynard's house, however, he learned that the old man had passed away two days earlier. On inquiring about the map, Denman learned that it, along with a trunk full of what were considered worthless papers, had been accidentally burned.

Despite the absence of a map, Denman entered the woods adjacent to the railroad tracks after crossing the Chattahoochee River and undertook the first of many searches. Like Maynard before him, Denman had no success.

The story of the lost $100,000 Cobb County gold cache has long since entered the realm of regional folklore. Many know the tale, and it has been estimated that, over the years, hundreds have searched for the treasure.

In 1970, a man who collected and researched such lore undertook a search for this particular lost treasure. After several attempts, he located the tree with the "M" and "X" markings emblazoned on the trunk. The cuts, now more than one hundred years old, were barely discernible; he only noticed them because they were highlighted by the angle of the setting sun. To this day, no one knows the significance of the letters.

According to the finder, the area around the tree had changed considerably since the burying of the gold. There was no evidence of the spring, which had apparently dried up. Dense underbrush had grown up throughout the region, making movement through the forest difficult. In addition, erosion had altered the landscape markedly during the previous century. Though the man has returned to the blazed tree dozens of times, he has been unable to locate the cache of gold coins.

In recent years, interest in the Cobb County gold cache has grown. It has been estimated that, if found today, the cache of gold coins would be worth several million dollars.

CHAPTER THREE

The Lost Treasure of
Colonel Norman Frisby

AT THE ONSET OF THE CIVIL WAR, COLONEL NORMAN FRISBY WAS regarded as one of the most successful and wealthy plantation operators in the South. His forty-two-thousand-acre farm stretched along north-eastern Louisiana's Tensas River for twenty-five miles. The Frisby plantation was known as a model of agricultural efficiency and productivity. According to histories of the region, Frisby owned over five hundred slaves, more than any other slaveholder in the United States. According to area history and lore, there are two other significant facts regarding Frisby: he was one of the most hated men in Louisiana, and he buried a fortune in gold and silver coins somewhere on his property that has never been found and would be worth several million dollars in today's values.

The complete and true story of Colonel Frisby may never be known. No one knows where he came from. Sometime during the early 1850s, he arrived at a Mississippi cotton plantation owned by an uncle who hired him to oversee the operation. Under Frisby's supervision, the farming of cotton proceeded more efficiently than before, and profits were impressive.

Frisby was convinced that success resulted from hard work, especially the hard work of slaves. It was said that Frisby monitored the daily work of the slaves on horseback, pausing now and then to whip one or another that he felt was not giving his best effort.

With his uncle's permission, Frisby had nearby swamps drained and forests cleared and placed into agricultural production. He doubled the number of slaves and kept them working eighteen hours per day. Though often criticized, Frisby doubled the plantation's cotton production within two years, profits grew, and he and his uncle became wealthy.

Impressed with the fortune that could be made from growing and selling cotton, Frisby decided it was time to own his own farm. Following several months of searching, he located and purchased thousands of acres of rich bottomland in the Tensas River basin in northeastern Louisiana not far from the present-day town of Newlight.

Since his arrival in Louisiana, Frisby had conducted his affairs under a shroud of secrecy and mystery. Many wondered how he acquired enough money to purchase forty-two thousand acres of rich farmland. Stories surfaced that he had been a pirate and that much of his wealth came from the spoils of numerous raids conducted in the Gulf of Mexico. Others insisted Frisby had discovered a cache of buried treasure once hidden by the pirate Jean Lafitte.

There is no record of how Frisby acquired the rank of colonel. There likewise exists no record of his service in the military of the United States. Many are convinced that his title was simply self-bestowed and that he began introducing himself in that manner when he first arrived in Louisiana.

Frisby was known to be cruel to his slaves, and a cemetery on his property held the bodies of many that had died from overwork in their chains. Others, it was said, were murdered, starved, or whipped to death by Frisby himself. In spite of his clandestine and suspicious manner, politicians currying favor and donations often praised Frisby as a man of vision and a progressive-minded citizen.

A wealthy man when he arrived in Louisiana, Frisby amassed a second fortune from his agricultural enterprises. It was his practice to convert all income into silver coins, which he stored in wooden kegs in his house. When his cotton plantation began to turn a hefty profit, Frisby took a wife. Within two years, he sired two daughters.

At first, the Frisby family lived in a three-room cabin on the property. With the birth of his second daughter, however, Frisby undertook the construction of an extravagant thirty-room mansion atop the highest elevation of the plantation. The new residence featured doorknobs and other fittings made from gold and silver, silver window frames, and gold and silver light fixtures. Mrs. Frisby ordered custom-made gold dinnerware. At one point, Frisby carried two hundred pounds of gold coins to New York City where they were melted down and fashioned into a bell that was eventually hung in front of the mansion to announce visitors.

In spite of his attempts at becoming an important member of Louisiana high society, Frisby's neighbors never accepted him. Some found the colonel lacking in the necessary social skills. Most considered him arrogant and abrasive. Though it was not uncommon to own slaves in those days, a number of northern Louisiana's citizens openly criticized Frisby's cruel treatment of his workers.

The rejection and exclusion bothered Frisby deeply, and he soon came to resent, even despise, his neighbors. In turn, they shunned him even more. Such behavior infuriated Frisby, and his relations along Tensas Creek grew more strained with each passing week.

Frisby's closest neighbor was a man named Flowers, who also happened to be his brother-in-law. Among other agricultural pursuits, Flowers raised mules, which he allowed to roam free and unfenced. From time to time the mules would wander onto Frisby's property to dine on the tender tops of young cotton plants. Frisby, aware of this, would herd the mules back onto Flowers's land and caution his brother-in-law about letting them run loose. One morning, on encountering two of Flowers's mules once again in his cotton, however, Frisby flew into a rage and shot both of them.

Not content with killing the mules, Frisby rode directly to Flowers's house, called him out onto the porch, and cursed and demeaned him in front of his wife and children. Flowers pulled a pistol from his belt, pointed it at Frisby, and ordered him away. Flowers told the colonel that if he ever returned he would be killed. Frisby left, swearing revenge.

During the following weeks, Frisby took his anger out on his slaves, working and whipping them without mercy. A number of them escaped and sought refuge at neighboring plantations, where they related the horrors of life on the Frisby farm.

As the Civil War gained momentum, Frisby grew concerned about the safety of his fortune. Like many Southerners of the day, Frisby had little confidence in banks and kept his wealth—in the form of gold and silver coins—in his mansion. When he became convinced that his fortune was in jeopardy from raiding Union forces, he decided to bury it in some secret location near his home. While he was pondering this, Frisby learned that the Louisiana legislature was considering a bill to abolish slavery. The bill, he discovered, was drafted in response to his treatment of slaves.

With these unsettling prospects at hand, Frisby decided to transport most of his slaves to Texas, where he knew he would be able to sell them at a good profit. Several weeks later, he returned to his plantation considerably richer, having accepted only gold coins for the sale of the slaves. As he added these new coins to his already impressive fortune, Frisby was informed of news that war was imminent.

Convinced that his wealth, known to all in the area, would attract Yankee raiders, Frisby was now more determined than ever to find a new location for it, one that could never be found. After informing his wife of his plans, he ordered a pair of his remaining slaves to load two kegs of gold and silver coins onto a wagon hitched to a team of mules. Added to these were the gold and silver fixtures, as well as the dinnerware, from the house. In a second wagon, he loaded the huge golden bell. Seating himself in one of the wagons, Frisby ordered the slaves to follow in the other. He drove the wagon down the trail toward the swampy lowlands. A short time later, the wagons and mules struggled through the muddy and yielding soil. When they could proceed no farther, Frisby ordered the slaves to unload everything from the wagons and bury it at that location. With difficulty, a hole was excavated. All of Frisby's wealth was placed into it.

After the hole was filled up and covered over, Frisby asked the two slaves if they thought they could ever return to the location. One said he couldn't, but the other insisted he could. Frisby stepped forward, grabbed the slave, and broke his neck. He let the body fall upon the freshly filled hole.

Frisby returned to his mansion with the remaining terrified slave following in the second wagon. On the way, the colonel spotted one of

Flowers's mules in his cotton field. The colonel reached into the back of the wagon, seized his rifle, and shot the animal. Deciding it was time to deal with Flowers once and for all, Frisby set out for his brother-in-law's home.

When Frisby's wagon had gone around a bend and was out of sight, the slave drove the second wagon directly to his shack, loaded up his family and their few belongings, and fled to Texas. He was never seen again.

On arriving at Flowers's home, Frisby was informed by the housekeeper that the family was attending a community picnic at Flowers Landing on the Tensas River. Realizing that he and his family had not been invited to the event further enraged the unstable Frisby. He drove the wagon toward the landing.

Screaming and cursing Flowers, Frisby steered the wagon into the midst of the gathered families. Spotting his brother-in-law among the crowd, Frisby retrieved his whip from the bed of the vehicle and attacked him. After receiving several violent lashes, Flowers was able to grab the whip and pull Frisby toward him. At the same time, he seized a long knife he had just employed to cut some meat and plunged it repeatedly into Frisby's chest. The colonel slumped to the ground and died within minutes.

Frisby and the second slave were the only two people who had knowledge of the secret location of the treasure. With Frisby dead and the slave gone to Texas, the location of the cache of gold and silver and other valuable items remained a mystery.

Within weeks, the Civil War arrived in Louisiana. Learning of Colonel Frisby's immense wealth in gold and silver coins, Union soldiers dug dozens of holes in the yard around the mansion. Inside the structure, they pulled up floors and pulled down walls in a fruitless attempt at locating the gold and silver.

Following years of skirmish and hardship, the war finally ended, but the South was no longer the same. Most plantations were unable to operate as before, and many were abandoned. Today, little remains of the Frisby mansion. The once-prosperous property has gone through a series of owners over the decades but remains active and productive.

On the margins of the fertile farmland lie areas of marshland and swamp, bottomlands thick with mosquitoes and water moccasins. Somewhere in this sodden, muddy environment lies, in today's values, millions of dollars' worth of gold and silver coins and other valuable items, a fortune waiting to be recovered.

CHAPTER FOUR

The Lost Parlange Fortune

CHARLES PARLANGE GREW UP IN A MANSION ON THE FAMILY SUGAR-cane plantation in Louisiana during the years following the Civil War. Charles was a frail boy who eschewed the out-of-doors and any kind of labor. His mother, Madame Virginie Parlange, was a widow and remained protective of the lad. Not interested in the opportunities for responsibility or hard work that could be found on the plantation, Charles turned instead to books, reading the entire collection of classics in the family library. Always studious, Charles excelled in school. When he was old enough, he went away to college to study law. He eventually married and had a son, Walter. With the passage of years, Charles was appointed a justice of the Supreme Court of Louisiana.

During his pursuit of a career in law, Charles was delivered the news of the death of his mother. After attending to the details of her funeral, he closed up the mansion and rarely returned to it. The building, as well as the plantation, lay abandoned for twenty years.

Unlike his father, the young Walter Parlange was fascinated with the tales of the mansion and the plantation. He was equally charmed and enchanted by stories of his grandmother. When he was grown, Walter decided to move into the mansion, and it was only after he had resided there for many years that he learned of the buried treasure.

During the Civil War, Virginie Parlange owned and managed the huge plantation near the town of New Roads in southern Louisiana, some

Charles Parlange
PEE WEE KOLB

thirty miles northwest of Baton Rouge. Madame Parlange was a widow, and her late husband had left her a fortune estimated to be worth half a million dollars in gold and silver coins.

During the height of conflict in Louisiana, word reached Madame Parlange that Union troops were on their way to her plantation. Knowing of the soldiers' propensity for looting, Parlange decided it would be prudent to gather up her fortune, along with many priceless furnishings, and hide them. After removing several wallboards, she stuffed her finest silver, china, and jewelry into the spaces and replaced the planks. She had her furniture carried into the attic and covered with quilts.

A number of leather pouches containing the family fortune in gold and silver coins were placed in three substantial wooden chests. This done, Madame Parlange ordered two of her most trusted servants to drag the chests out to the garden and bury them. She watched as the chests were placed in three different and widely separated excavations and the holes filled in. Following this, she returned to her mansion to await the arrival of the Union forces.

A short time later, a contingent of Yankee soldiers rode into the great yard in front of the mansion. Seated astride their mounts, they admired the structure that had originally been built by the Marquis Vincent de Ternant in 1750. It was surrounded by groves of live oak and pecan trees. Beyond the groves stretched vast fields of sugarcane.

Madame Parlange stepped out onto the front porch, greeted the soldiers, and invited them to dinner. They accepted, and she was treated with courtesy by the troops. They informed her that they wished to camp on her property for several days, and she pointed to a suitable location where firewood and water were available. Several days later, they thanked her for her hospitality and rode away. Concerned that other squads of Union cavalry would arrive at the plantation, Madame Parlange decided to leave the treasure buried in the garden until the war was over.

Years passed, and when it became safe to assume hostilities were drawing to a close, Madame Parlange, with the help of her slaves, undertook the work of restoring the mansion and the plantation to their former glory. The furnishings that had been stored in the attic were carried down and returned to their original places. The silver, china, and jewelry were retrieved from the hiding places in the walls, thoroughly cleaned, and placed into use once again.

Deciding it was time to dig up the three chests filled with gold and silver coins, Madame Parlange led her son, Charles, out to the garden and showed him where to dig the first hole. With difficulty accompanied by complaint, the boy excavated several inches into the ground and struck the first chest. After removing more of the dirt, he and his mother managed to wrestle the heavy chest from the ground and drag it into the mansion.

Several yards away, a second chest was unearthed and retrieved. When Madame Parlange directed Charles to the third location, however, no chest was found. More excavations ensued, yet no chest could be located. Charles, exhausted from the unaccustomed labor, begged for

Parlange Plantation House
PEE WEE KOLB

relief. Despite his protestations, over the next several days he was directed by his mother to excavate several more holes in search of the third chest. It could not be found.

Finally, Madame Parlange summoned the two slaves who had helped her bury the three chests only to discover that they no longer lived on the plantation. She learned later that they had departed for Texas to live with relatives.

Following the war, the Parlange plantation fell on hard times. With no slaves to work in the cane fields, and with Charles preparing to leave for law school, Madame Parlange resigned herself to living the remainder of her days alone in the mansion.

According to documents encountered by Walter in later years, the missing chest contained gold and silver coins worth $100,000 in 1860 values. Walter decided he would attempt to locate the chest for himself. It proved to be more difficult than he imagined. Despite all his efforts, he was never able to identify the location of the original garden where the chest was buried. Though he persisted in his search off and on for several years, he finally gave up.

During the 1950s, professional treasure hunters were allowed onto the property to try to locate the missing chest. Though the original garden plot was never located, several holes were dug on the property, but nothing was ever found. According to surviving members of the Parlange family, the chest containing the fortune in gold and silver coins is still buried somewhere on the land not far from the old mansion. It has been suggested that state-of-the-art metal detectors and other gold- and silver-locating technology could be employed to recover the treasure with some promise of success. To date, however, no organized attempts have been made.

CHAPTER FIVE

Sunken Confederate Treasure and Arms off the South Carolina Coast

WHEN THE WAR BETWEEN THE STATES BEGAN GAINING IMPETUS IN 1861, England maintained an official position of neutrality. Secretly, however, the British government supported the South. As the momentum of the war increased, many representatives of the British government as well as a number of private citizens aligned themselves with the philosophies of the secessionist Confederacy. In addition, several prominent British industrialists had invested heavily in the American South; therefore, supporting the Rebel cause remained in their best interests.

As a result of the British investment in the American Civil War, particularly in the South, several organizations were formed in England that were devoted to accumulating and shipping arms, ammunition, and money to the Southern effort. In this manner, an active supply program for the Confederates was instituted.

The British provided ships to carry weapons and money to the South on a continuing basis. So regular were the shipments, however, that in time the ongoing plot to supply the Confederates was detected by Union forces. As a result, Yankee warships regularly patrolled the Atlantic side of the American coast from Florida to Virginia. On occasion, the Union warships sailed as far as the West Indies, where they would intercept a British supply ship from time to time. During one such encounter, which became known as the Trent Affair, a second war was nearly precipitated between the United States and Great Britain.

The *York Castle*
PEE WEE KOLB

At the height of the Civil War, as many as thirty British ships were regularly crossing and recrossing the Atlantic Ocean, carrying supplies and funds to the Southerners. Now and then one of these vessels would encounter a Union blockade and be turned away, but many managed to reach some port along the coast to deliver their valuable cargo.

In April 1863, the British warship *York Castle* lay moored to a dock at a London port location. For three days and nights, a contingent of both British and American sailors worked to prepare the ship for a trans-Atlantic crossing. Contrary to official British policy, the cargo hold was filled with a secret consignment bound for the southern United States. The shipment, contributed by several British organizations in sympathy with the Confederate cause, consisted of 1,300 Enfield rifles, twenty-four kegs of black powder, several crates of ammunition, and $350,000 worth of gold ingots. When the cargo had finally been loaded and the ship readied, the *York Castle* slipped quietly from the dock, through the harbor, and out to sea.

The *York Castle* was a corvette—a small, fast warship. The primary advantage of such a vessel was speed, an important factor when trying to evade Union blockades and outrun pursuing ships. One drawback, however, was related to the fact that, because of its small size, the corvette carried only a few light canons. This proved to be a distinct disadvantage during armed engagements with larger battleships.

Following an uneventful crossing of a portion of the ocean, the *York Castle* arrived at the islands of the Bahamas to take on fresh food and water. The Bahamas, an archipelago located in the Atlantic Ocean south-east of Florida, were a common stopover point for ships from Europe and elsewhere to replenish supplies and rest their crews. In addition, information regarding the location of Union warships was often available.

During the time the *York Castle* was docked at Grand Bahamas Island, the captain learned from the officers and crew of other British blockade-runners that most of the Yankee ships had been pulled out of Southern waters. After remaining in port for two days, the captain of the *York Castle* decided it was safe to set sail for Virginia, where a contingent of Rebel soldiers awaited the shipment of gold and weapons.

On arriving just off the east coast of Florida, the *York Castle* sailed northward, staying close to the shore. Should a Union warship be spotted, the swift corvette was capable of sailing up a shallow estuary, thereby evading confrontation. For several days, the captain of the corvette believed he was piloting the only vessel in these waters, for not a single ship had been spotted. The captain began to relax, believing the rest of the voyage was destined to go smoothly.

This was not the case. After crossing Winyah Bay between South Carolina's North Island and South Island, two Union ships suddenly appeared. The captain of the British corvette decided to try to outrun the Union ships when he noticed that they were cutters. Like the corvette, cutters were swift and maneuverable on the open sea.

Within minutes, it was clear that the *York Castle* would be overtaken. The British captain positioned the corvette such that it could fire its canons at the approaching cutters. The first volley struck one of the Union ships and rendered it useless for further action. The other cutter, however, returned fire and succeeded in destroying the corvette's mast. The heavy sails caught fire and tumbled onto the foredeck, which likewise broke out in flames. As the inferno raged and several of the crew attempted to fight the blaze, the *York Castle*'s canons continued to fire on the cutter. Minutes later, however, the crew of the *York Castle* decided to abandon the destroyed ship and jumped into the water.

Several more minutes passed, and the flames sweeping across the British corvette reached the black powder stored in the hull. A tremendous explosion resulted, which lifted the entire ship out of the water. The front of the corvette had been completely blown apart, and shattered planks and timbers were hurled into the sea for more than one hundred yards in all directions. The destroyed vessel slammed back down onto the surface of the water, settled at an odd list for several seconds, and then slowly took on water and sank beneath the waves. A minute later, the cargo of $350,000 in gold ingots, along with the weapons and ammunition, rested on the bottom of the continental shelf.

The captain of the *York Castle* was killed in the blast. The functioning Yankee cutter rescued thirty survivors, all of whom were taken to the nearest port and placed under arrest.

Other than those who had arranged for the shipment of the arms and gold, along with the captain and a handful of the crew of the *York Castle*, few had been aware of the cargo that was being transported. As far as the Union was concerned, the corvette was regarded as nothing more than another casualty of war and soon forgotten.

During the 1920s, however, while examining some obscure documents in England, a researcher uncovered pertinent information concerning the secret mission and cargo of the *York Castle*. Following verification of the data, the researcher decided to attempt to salvage the treasure. An expedition was organized, and within months the continental shelf east of South Carolina's North Island was searched for the remains of the treasure-laden British corvette. Because the exact location of the sinking was never precisely recorded, the salvage team conducted a systematic grid search of the sea floor near North Island. During the search, however, a heavy storm blew up from the ocean and caused the team to abandon the quest. For several weeks, the seas around North Island remained choppy and hazardous. Finally, after running out of funds and patience, the expedition team gave up and returned to England.

A thorough search of existing documents suggests that no other organized attempt at locating the remains of the *York Castle* was ever conducted. Should the corvette be found, the cargo of gold, worth millions of dollars today, along with hundreds of antique Enfield rifles, will be found lying among the ruins.

CHAPTER SIX

The Treasure in the Well

IN THE SOUTHWESTERN PART OF TENNESSEE'S MADISON COUNTY, there exists some acreage that old-timers still refer to as the Old Fuller Place. Artie Fuller purchased the land a short time prior to the onset of the War between the States. Fuller, a middle-aged man, married with no children, a successful cotton farmer and businessman, constructed an impressive mansion on the property and was reputed to be one of the wealthiest citizens of Tennessee.

Fuller's cotton plantation thrived, his harvests always bountiful. He insisted that payment for his crop be made in gold coin, which he stuffed into canvas sacks. As the profits from his cotton plantation grew, so did his distrust of banks. It was said that he stored his wealth in the mansion's closets, piling his sacks of gold among the shoes and boots.

As the Civil War raged throughout the South, Madison County was spared many of the horrors that were heaped onto other places. Though both Union and Confederate troops were regularly spotted riding through the region, Madison County citizens remained relatively unmolested.

With the help of his slaves, Fuller was able to go about the business of growing and harvesting cotton during the conflict. A practical businessman, Fuller regarded the Civil War as a temporary nuisance. A rabid supporter of the Confederacy, he hated Yankees above all else. He firmly believed that the South would prevail and that the forces of the North would be driven from the region, never to return. Life, he assured himself, would go back to normal.

On the morning of June 10, 1864, Fuller's wife, Jessie, insisted that he remove his sacks of gold coins from the closets and find a different location for them. She needed the closet space, she explained, for other things. Enlisting the help of one of his slaves, Fuller carried all the sacks out onto the front porch. He dismissed the slave, made himself a drink, and sat down in a nearby chair to contemplate a proper secret location for his wealth.

As Fuller was pondering this, a horseman approached the mansion, whipping his mount with passion. Reining to a halt in front of the mansion's porch, the rider warned Fuller of approaching Yankee troopers and then sped away. Fuller, not wanting the Union soldiers to see his gold, grew frantic. He was aware of the Northern soldiers' penchant for raiding and confiscating anything of value. Since Fuller's standing as a wealthy plantation owner was well known throughout the region, he had no doubt that the Yankees had learned of his home cache of gold coins. Fuller summoned his slave once again, and in the few minutes before the mounted troops arrived, the two carried the sacks of gold coins to the nearby well and tossed them in as Jessie Fuller watched from the front porch of the mansion. As the final sack splashed into the waters, a contingent of fifteen armed and uniformed men rode up the path toward the house.

As the newcomers approached, Fuller realized at a glance that they were not soldiers at all but bandits. Though clothed in the garb of Union troops, they were little more than a ragtag band of scruffy outlaws. Like many others of the time, these desperate men made a living raiding and looting small towns and area farms. They were also known to torture and kill citizens in the process. Fuller ran into the mansion just as the riders pulled up in front of his porch.

The leader of the band was a man named Fielding Hurst. Hurst was known as a bloodthirsty cutthroat and was wanted by both Union and Confederate forces alike as well as by several law enforcement agencies. Hurst had served time with the Confederate army. After being discharged, he joined the Union army and shortly thereafter deserted. At the time, Hurst was the most wanted man in western Tennessee.

In the house, Fuller ordered his wife, the maid, and the cook to take shelter in the cellar. This done, Fuller grabbed a shotgun and stepped out

The Hanging of Artie Fuller
PEE WEE KOLB

onto the porch to face the bandits. Summoning all of his courage, he pointed the shotgun at Hurst and ordered him and his followers off of the property immediately.

Remaining seated upon his horse, Hurst engaged Fuller in conversation as two members of his gang slipped from their mounts and crept toward the farmer from the sides. At a signal from Hurst, the two outlaws jumped on Fuller, snatched the shotgun from his grasp, and wrestled him to the ground. Dismounting, Hurst walked up to the helpless plantation owner and demanded he turn over his fortune immediately. When Fuller refused, he was kicked several times in the ribs. This done, Hurst explained he would ask one more time, and if Fuller refused he would be killed.

Hurst asked again, and again the farmer refused. Enraged, Hurst ordered two of his henchmen to drag Fuller to a nearby tree and prepare to hang him. A noose was fashioned and secured around the farmer's neck, and the other end was thrown over a stout branch. At a command from Hurst, several of the bandits grabbed the trailing end of the rope and lifted Fuller several feet off the ground. Fuller fought the tightening noose with an energy that belied his age but soon passed out. Hurst instructed his men to let go of the rope, and Fuller dropped to the ground. Several minutes later, when Fuller regained consciousness, Hurst asked him again to reveal the location of his gold. Gasping for breath and barely able to speak as a result of the constriction of his throat by the noose, Fuller told Hurst to go to hell.

For a second time, Hurst ordered Fuller hoisted into the air, and as before Fuller struggled until passing out once again. When his exertions ceased, Fuller was lowered to the ground, barely alive. Once more, Hurst demanded that Fuller turn over his gold. The farmer shook his head and cursed the outlaw. For a third time, Fuller was pulled up and left dangling by the rope. This time, Hurst let him hang until he was dead.

As two of the outlaws tied off the rope and left the corpse swinging from the tree limb, Hurst led the rest of the outlaws into the house to ransack it. For hours they searched the mansion, the barn, and several outbuildings but found none of Fuller's gold. Jessie Fuller, along with the hired help, went undiscovered in their cellar hideaway.

Later, when it was apparent that the outlaws had departed, Jessie, the maid, and the cook came out from hiding. Jessie found her dead husband and cut him down. Three days later, Fuller was buried on his plantation.

For weeks following the funeral, Jessie Fuller remained at the mansion and pondered her future. She decided she no longer cared to remain in Madison County and made arrangements to go live with her sister in Holly Springs, Mississippi.

While making preparations to leave the plantation, Jessie would visit the well several times each day and peer into its depths as though pondering what to do about the great fortune in gold coin hidden there. A few days prior to leaving for Mississippi, she asked the slaves to fill in the shaft and remove any and all evidence of the existence of the well. When her neighbors asked why she did such a thing, she refused to discuss the matter and quickly changed the subject. Years later, when she was elderly, she was asked the same question. With the passage of so much time, Jessie Fuller felt no need to keep the secret any longer, so she told about the hiding of the gold from the outlaws. She simply concluded her tale by stating that the money belonged to her husband and that no one else should have it.

With the passing of more years, the story of Artie Fuller's treasure in the well became known throughout the Tennessee south. Hopeful searchers arrived at the old plantation and conducted searches for evidence of the location of the old well. Several excavations were made in the yard in front of the mansion, but nothing was ever found.

After Jessie Fuller departed Madison County, the mansion and the plantation remained abandoned. By 1921, the house had fallen into such a state of disrepair that it was torn down. The razing of the building was attended by dozens of nearby residents who poked through the debris and around the foundation in hope of finding some of Fuller's old coins.

Today, the story of Fuller's treasure in the well is familiar to many throughout the American South. Though the gold coins have been searched for by many over the years, the hopeful continue to arrive at the old plantation to continue the quest. With luck and perseverance, the foundation of the old mansion can still be found. Somewhere in the front yard a short distance away is the location of the old well and a fortune in gold coins estimated to be worth several million dollars in today's values. How deep in the ground the gold lies can only be guessed at, but it is apparently well beyond the range of most commercially available high-tech metal detectors. There exist other methods for locating gold deep underground, however, and it may just be a matter of time before newer and more sophisticated gold-locating equipment is brought onto the old Fuller plantation.

CHAPTER SEVEN

Lost Yankee Payroll

DURING THE CIVIL WAR, BOTH UNION AND CONFEDERATE FORCES remained constantly on the move throughout selected portions of the American South. The state of Tennessee saw as much traffic as any other. Along with men, horses, mules, artillery, wagons, supplies, and more, the armies of the North and South carried payrolls. Payment, both in currency and coin, was passed out on paydays to the soldiers while on the march. It is estimated that at any given time during the war, payrolls amounting to millions of dollars were in transit from one skirmish to another, from one campsite to another.

In December 1862, Union Colonel C. L. Dunham, commander of the Thirty-Ninth Iowa Division, led mounted troops and foot soldiers into western Tennessee with the intention of engaging Confederate general Nathan Bedford Forrest and his Seventh Tennessee Cavalry. On December 29, Dunham's division, heading south, passed through the small Carroll County town of Huntington in the western part of the state.

Dunham was a newcomer in the territory with which Forrest was highly experienced. The Confederate general had considerable success in battles and skirmishes throughout that part of Tennessee. Dunham's most recent intelligence had Forrest's army camped at a location called Parker's Crossroads, located fifteen miles south of Huntington. Dunham received specific orders from General Ulysses S. Grant to proceed to Forrest's location, engage, and defeat the enemy.

By the time Dunham's command reached Clarksburg, ten miles south of Huntington, the sun had set. A few hundred yards out of town, one of the scouts found a freshwater spring and a suitable place to set up camp. Dunham directed his troopers toward the location, and within minutes tents were set up, horses and mules were unsaddled and hobbled, and cooking fires were started.

During the night, Dunham's scouts were sent forward to ascertain Forrest's exact location and the number of Rebel troops under his command. Reporting back just before dawn of the following day, the scouts informed the colonel that the Confederate command was, indeed, camped at Parker's Crossroads five miles away and due south. The Rebels were apparently aware of the approaching Union force, for they were spotted digging trenches and making other battle preparations.

Without taking time for breakfast, Dunham ordered his soldiers to ready their weapons and mounts for the march to Forrest's camp. As the troopers busied themselves with preparations for the coming battle, Dunham addressed the disposition of the payroll chest. Not wishing to risk its capture by the Union forces, Dunham decided to bury the chest, which contained $15,000 in coins. When the battle was over, Dunham intended to return to the campsite and retrieve the payroll. With the aid of two trusted lieutenants and one sergeant, Dunham alternately carried and dragged the heavy chest to a location two hundred feet east of the spring. Here a hole was excavated, the chest lowered into it, and the hole covered.

Unseen by the four men, a Union scout named Allen Chambliss was squatted on a low knoll overlooking the excavation site. As he smoked a cigarette and cleaned his rifle, Chambliss observed the caching of the payroll chest. This made a total of five men who had knowledge of the location of the buried coins.

For most of the day, Dunham's command advanced slowly and cautiously toward the Confederate encampment, taking extreme care to keep silent and unseen. By nightfall, the Yankees, hiding in the woods, could see the campfires and men moving about a few hundred yards away. Not wishing to engage the well-entrenched enemy in the dark, the members of the Thirty-Ninth Iowa Division fought for whatever sleep they could get, readying themselves for a strike on the Rebel camp at dawn.

Moments before sunrise on the morning of December 31, the first shots were fired from the Yankees in hiding, and the fight was on. For

Nathan Bedford Forrest
PEE WEE KOLB

nearly a full day, the two sides fought with both incurring heavy casualties. Dunham's command outnumbered the Confederates by a significant margin, but the canny Forrest managed to create mass confusion and heavy damage. Late in the day, and having accomplished all he believed was possible against Dunham's superior numbers, Forrest ordered his soldiers to retreat southwestward from the battle site. A short time later, they crossed the Tennessee River near the town of Clifton.

At the Parker's Crossroads battle site, nearly one hundred men, both Union and Confederate, lay dead. Hundreds more had suffered serious wounds, and during the next several days and nights, military surgeons treated the injured while squads of enlisted men buried the dead. Dunham looked on as the two lieutenants and the sergeant who helped him bury the payroll chest were lowered into the ground.

The tasks of treating the injured and burying the dead were not made any easier by the heavy rains that began to fall on the morning after the battle. The downpour lasted for seven days.

Among the Union soldiers recovering from wounds in one of the army tents was Allen Chambliss. He had been struck by a Rebel bullet during the first few minutes of the action, lost a great deal of blood, and was initially pronounced dead. On the third day after the battle, he regained consciousness, and the doctors believed his chances for a full recovery were good.

As Chambliss lay on his cot being tended to by medical aides, the battlefield had turned into a quagmire, and movement was restricted. On the morning of the sixth day, Dunham assembled a contingent of six well-armed men and a wagon and rode back toward Clarksburg with the intention of retrieving the payroll chest.

On two occasions they were forced to abandon the trail and hide from Rebel patrols. When they had reached a point two miles from their goal, they were fired on by a third enemy patrol, and two of the Union soldiers were killed. Finally, frustrated by the weather and the danger of Confederates in the area, Dunham decided to abandon the chest for the time being.

When the rain finally let up, Dunham led his command back toward the north, where he hoped to find a suitable place to rest men and horses and replenish supplies. Several of the most seriously wounded soldiers, including Chambliss, were taken to a makeshift hospital in Huntington to recover. While waiting in the town, Dunham received orders to assemble all his able-bodied soldiers and conduct an expedition into another region. With the formidable task of leading men into battle and securing victory for the North, Dunham eventually forgot about the buried payroll chest located near the spring just outside the town of Clarksburg. While recovering in the hospital, Chambliss could think of nothing but the buried treasure.

Three months passed before Chambliss recovered sufficiently from his wound to leave the hospital. Deciding not to rejoin his unit, the scout obtained a mount and rode south toward Clarksburg. His intention was to retrieve the payroll chest and return to his farm a much richer man than when he left.

On arriving, Chambliss was surprised to discover that the landscape surrounding the spring had changed dramatically. Heavy runoff from the torrential rains that had plagued Dunham's command for a full week had filled the nearby streams, creating flash floods. This, along with the increased overland runoff, eroded away tons of topsoil in some areas and deposited it in others. It was with difficulty that Chambliss finally found the actual location of the spring near where the Union soldiers had camped before engaging Forrest. He tied his horse to a bush and walked to the spot where he believed the chest had been buried. A wide hole was excavated, but nothing was found. Chambliss dug in another location with the same result. By the end of the day, at least a dozen holes had been dug, but the payroll chest remained elusive.

For several months, Chambliss camped near the spring and searched the area over and over for the buried chest but with no success. On several occasions he would walk to the low hill from which he'd observed the burial of the chest, but from his vantage point nothing looked the same as it had before the rains.

Over the years, Chambliss told the story of his search for the buried payroll chest, and in time the tale entered the annals of Tennessee folklore. A search of government records revealed that Dunham did, in fact, transport a payroll chest during his mission to engage General Forrest. What became of it was not recorded. When Dunham's personal journal was located, it was searched for information pertaining to the burying of the payroll chest, but no mention of the event was found. Because the busy commander had little time for making notations in his journal, he likewise made no mention of the routes he traveled or of the locations of campsites.

In spite of the fact that the Union payroll chest was buried a century and a half ago, people continue to search for it. To compound the difficulty in finding the chest, researchers have discovered there is not just one spring located in this area but as many as five. Which of the springs was the one near where Dunham buried the payroll chest remains a mystery.

CHAPTER EIGHT

Kegs of Gold and Silver Coins

COFFEE COUNTY, TENNESSEE, LOCATED NEAR THE SOUTHWESTERN end of the Cumberland Mountains, was never an easy place to make a living. The soil was too thin to raise a decent crop of anything, and the weather was too cold, too hot, too wet, or too dry. During the middle part of the nineteenth century, few souls lived in this remote area, and those who did were a hardy sort, a tough breed of survivors who, for the most part, shunned society, had few rules, and endured Indian and bandit raids, insect plagues, drought, and floods. Through it all, they somehow managed to plant and harvest a few basic crops and raise their families.

As if things weren't bad enough in Coffee County, it got worse during the Civil War. Patrols from both the Union and Confederate armies moved through the county, sometimes stopping at isolated villages and small farms and ordering residents to feed them. When the armies needed beef, soldiers were sent to steal and butcher livestock and raid gardens for produce. When the residents, few and poorly armed, tried to resist they were often killed.

Even worse than the military were the gangs of outlaws. During the last few months of the war, bands of renegade robbers and killers, often composed of deserters from both armies, roamed throughout much of Tennessee and routinely attacked and raided the defenseless settlements.

A man named Cephus Wenten had lived in Coffee County for many years. He and his family endured hardship along with everyone else, but he had not only survived but prospered. Having dealt successfully with soldiers from both the Yankee and Rebel armies, Wenten had no reason to believe he would not be able to prevail against ragtag gangs of outlaws.

Wenten was one of the few successful farmers in Coffee County. In the nearby town of Hillsboro, he was well respected for his dedication and hard work. Years of paying close attention to the labor and management of his farm resulted in good profits. Like most Southerners, Wenten was distrustful of banks and preferred to keep his money at home. Always insisting on payment in gold and silver coins, Wenten stashed his earnings over the years in three old wooden nail kegs that he in turn buried in the yard not far from his house. No one knew for certain how much money Wenten had, but reliable estimates place it at $55,000.

One afternoon in 1864, a group of men rode onto the Wenten farm. When Cephus walked out to greet them, they pulled guns and pointed them at the farmer. Wenten recognized the men as a ragged band of outlaws known locally as the Brixie gang. They explained to Wenten that they had just come from Hillsboro where they learned about his gold and silver coins stored in kegs. They further instructed Wenten to retrieve his fortune and turn it over to them immediately.

Wenten refused, and two of the outlaws dismounted and beat him with their pistols until he was unconscious and his head a bloody mess. When Wenten regained consciousness, they again told him to turn over his gold and silver, but still he refused. Wenten's hands were tied behind his back, a noose placed around his neck, and the end of the rope tossed over a low-hanging limb. The outlaws threatened to hang him if he did not produce his money. Still, Wenten refused. At a command from the leader of the gang, two of the outlaws pulled on the rope, lifting the farmer several inches off the ground. As Wenten kicked and struggled against the constricting noose, the two men tied the rope off to the trunk of the tree. Moments later, the farmer was dead.

Mrs. Wenten was discovered hiding in the nearby woods. She was dragged to where her dead husband hung from the tree and thrown to the ground. The outlaws told her she would also die if she did not reveal the location of Wenten's fortune. Mrs. Wenten panicked and began screaming for her life and struggling against the grip of her captors. She knew she was going to die, for her husband had never informed her of where he buried his treasure. Aggravated with the screaming woman and low on patience, one of the outlaws shot Mrs. Wenten in the head, killing her instantly.

While ransacking the house, the outlaws encountered three of the Wenten children in hiding. Each was given the opportunity to reveal the location of the gold and silver coins, but like their mother, they were ignorant of the cache. All three were killed.

For the remainder of the day, the outlaws dug holes near the house in search of the treasure. Finding none, they mounted up and rode away.

One day in 1924, a man accidentally discovered a portion of the Wenten treasure. While exploring around the old abandoned farm, he spotted the top edge of what appeared to be a small wooden barrel sticking out of the ground in the lot behind the sagging, listing farmhouse. After removing some of the dirt from around it, he managed to pull the heavy object out of the hole. The wood was partially rotted, so it was with little difficulty that the finder broke open the top and peered inside. Initially unbelieving of what his eyes told him, he spilled the contents onto the ground and stared at a fortune in gold and silver coins.

Nervous that he might have accidentally stumbled onto someone's buried cache, the man looked around to see if he was being observed. Carefully, he replaced the coins into the keg, dropped it back into the hole, and covered it up. He returned to his home and pondered his discovery.

For years, the man stayed away from the Wenten farm and never told anyone about his find. He was tempted to dig up the fortune in gold and silver coins and keep them for himself but was never certain it was the right thing to do. He was convinced the coins were someone else's property and that it would be wrong for him to take them.

One day, however, he decided to tell his secret to a close friend named Peter Cunningham. Cunningham thought about the hidden cache of coins for a full year and, having far fewer scruples about such things than his friend, decided to go dig them up for himself. For a full week he made plans to go to the old Wenten farm. He collected digging tools, a canteen of water, and good hiking shoes. Unfortunately for Cunningham, on the day before he was to leave on his quest, he suffered a stroke and died a few days later.

Many who live in the foothills of the Cumberland Plateau region are familiar with the tale of Cephus Wenten's buried coin cache. They are also aware that the man who found the coins in 1924 located only one of the three kegs in which the treasure was stored. A few have been tempted to search for the treasure, but most are deterred because of an additional curious element to the story. It is the belief of some that there is a curse associated with the Wenten treasure. They claim that the ghosts of Cephus Wenten, his wife, and his three murdered children stand guard over the gold and silver coins. Any who attempt to locate and retrieve the treasure, they believe, risk losing their lives to the curse.

CHAPTER NINE

Lost Confederate Payroll

FIVE CONFEDERATE SOLDIERS RODE WITH EXTREME CAUTION THROUGH a densely wooded area of a remote portion of the Ozark Mountains in northwestern Arkansas. Uneasy, they cast furtive glances into the thick forest, ever on the lookout for a Yankee patrol. The leader of the small military contingent was a sergeant, a veteran of several Civil War skirmishes. He peered into the shadowy foliage, ever watchful, ever listening. Now and then he looked back at the men in his detachment—three privates and one corporal. The sergeant was wishing he had been provided with seasoned soldiers instead of these four raw recruits.

The sergeant had been given the responsibility of delivering a large payroll to the Confederate encampment near Prairie Grove, a few miles northeast of Fayetteville and several miles farther up the trail. Before he departed, the sergeant was warned by his commanding officer that Union troops were in the area. Because of a shortage of qualified men, he explained, the sergeant would have to deliver the payroll without the normal contingent of guards.

As the soldiers rode north along the old military road, the sergeant regarded his four charges. The corporal was barely more than a boy but had proven himself eager and competent. He had been given the responsibility of leading the packhorse on which the military payroll was strapped—bags of gold coins with which to pay the soldiers at Prairie Grove. Like the sergeant, he too scanned the woods for any sign of the enemy.

The three privates were visibly nervous about the assignment. They were all seventeen years of age or younger. They had been in the army for less than four months, and none had seen action.

The sergeant had turned in his saddle to check the fastenings on the payroll bags when a shot rang out from the trees to the right of the detachment. The bullet struck him in the chest, knocking him from his horse. As he hit the ground, he screamed, "Ambush!" Then he died. Several more shots were fired in rapid succession from a hiding place, and two of the privates fell from their mounts, dead before they hit the ground.

The third private was also hit but had the presence of mind to hang on to his saddle as he spurred his mount up the trail toward Prairie Grove. His wound was serious, however, and before he traveled fifty yards he passed out and fell from his horse.

Both the corporal and his horse were in a panic. The young man was desperately trying to control his excited mount while at the same time maintaining a grip on the reins of the packhorse transporting the payroll. As a result, he was unable to pull his pistol to return fire. After a few moments amid the shooting and shouting, the corporal managed to turn his horse and spur it back in the direction from which the detachment had just come. Fearing pursuit by Union soldiers, he ran the horses at top speed until it seemed as if they could go no farther.

A mile and a half down the trail, the corporal stopped to rest the animals. He listened for sign or sound of pursuit, but there was none. As he sat astride his horse studying the trail and woods, he spied a shallow horizontal opening in a limestone bluff several yards off the trail. Assuming the Yankees would be arriving at any moment, the corporal dismounted, pulled the payroll sacks from the packhorse, and stashed them in the crevice at the base of the cliff. Following this, he stuffed rocks, branches, and other debris into the crack to make it appear much as the rest of the forest floor. This done, he ran to his horse, mounted up, and, leading the unladen packhorse, returned to his company to report the attack.

When the corporal arrived back at the encampment, he found it in turmoil. Men were dashing to and fro securing rifles, ammunition, and provisions and preparing their mounts for a forced ride. He sought out

Rebel Corporal Fleeing with Payroll
PEE WEE KOLB

the company commander and reported the attack on the payroll detachment, escaping the ambush, and concealing the gold payroll beside the trail during his return.

The commander made a few notes on the matter in his journal and then informed the corporal that attending to the payroll would have to wait for another time. The company had just received orders to prepare to engage a force of Union soldiers at Prairie Grove. Within the hour, the entire Confederate company was on the march back up the trail. During the ride, the corporal related his recent experience and the caching of the gold payroll in a rock crevice to several of the troopers.

The fight at Prairie Grove is regarded as one of the major Civil War battles to take place in Arkansas. The corporal, along with many other Confederate soldiers, was killed during the action that ensued. A few of the soldiers who had heard the corporal's story of caching the payroll recalled the tale months and years after being mustered out of the army. All attempted to locate the cache. None were successful.

The old military trace that led to Prairie Grove from the south can be found on historical maps of the area. At several locations along this road can be found exposed limestone bluffs. According to most of the research conducted on this tale, the sacks of gold coins are still cached in a hidden limestone crevice at the base of one of the cliffs.

CHAPTER TEN

The Lipscomb Plantation Treasure

As a result of a growing market for cotton, along with an abundance of slave labor, a number of large plantations became established throughout the fertile American South during the 1840s and 1850s. As the market grew, so did the demand for laborers.

A prosperous Georgia farmer named Lipscomb operated a big plantation near the town of La Grange, a growing settlement in the western part of the state near the Alabama border. Ever the enterprising businessman, Lipscomb believed he could make a lot of money by supplying slaves to other plantation owners.

Lipscomb's plantation, along with his newly developed slave trade, flourished. In a few short years, he amassed a fortune amounting to $100,000 in profits, a great deal of money at the time.

Banks were scarce in the developing South, and the few that could be found suffered from far too many inconsistencies in accounting and were susceptible to robbery. Lipscomb, like so many other farmers and businessmen of the day, distrusted banks and preferred to hide his money on his own property. With the help of a trusted slave, an elderly white-haired black man named Sledge, Lipscomb cached a total of $100,000 in gold and silver coins in two separate locations in the yard in front of his house.

From time to time, Lipscomb would add to his hoard. Late at night, when his family was asleep, he would quietly leave the house and tiptoe to the slave quarters, where he would awaken Sledge and order him to dig into one of the caches. Here, Lipscomb would deposit his most recent profits. Lipscomb's wife and children were aware that he possessed a great amount of money, but they had no idea where it was hidden, and he would not tell them.

When the Civil War broke out, Lipscomb feared it would interfere with his slave trade business should the North be victorious. As the war progressed, it became clear that the South was going to lose. These concerns, along with his advanced age and deteriorating health, plunged Lipscomb into a spiral of depression and despair from which he never emerged. He began to neglect his family and farm. His only interest appeared to be centered on his buried fortune.

From time to time, with the help of Sledge, Lipscomb would dig up his money, and for hours he would sit on the ground and handle the gold and silver coins. It was the only thing that seemed to bring him pleasure.

One evening Lipscomb decided to count his coins. He went in search of Sledge but was unable to find him. He grew frantic when he realized that without the help of the black man he was unable to locate his two caches. All night long the distressed Lipscomb dug holes in his yard trying to locate his treasure, all to no avail. The next morning, he was found lying on the ground clutching a shovel. He was shaking, exhausted, and delirious.

Later that same day, when Lipscomb was a bit more lucid, he concocted a plan that would assure him of being able to find his fortune anytime he wished. He decided to record the locations of the buried coins and then hide the directions in a place known only to him.

After finding Sledge and enlisting his assistance, Lipscomb located the two caches and placed a small stake in the ground above each one. Taking a heavy, ornamental lead plate from his wife's buffet, he carried it to a point in the front yard between the house and the well. From where he stood, Lipscomb could see the two stakes.

Next, he withdrew a gold coin from his pocket and hammered it into the center of one side of the plate. With a penknife, he etched a soft arrow into the lead that pointed in the direction of the first cache. He then etched the number of paces to the site from where he stood. Turning the plate over, he then hammered a silver coin into the opposite side and recorded a directional arrow along with the number of steps to the second treasure. After scraping out a shallow hole in the ground at his feet, the plantation owner buried the plate so that each arrow pointed precisely in the direction of the respective treasure troves. Lipscomb told himself he would never have to worry again about finding his treasure.

Weeks passed, and Lipscomb became more paranoid about the possibility of Union soldiers coming to his farm and seizing his treasure. He imagined that Yankee troops numbering in the thousands were riding toward his plantation with the intention of taking his money from him. He even began to suspect Sledge of being in league with the thieving Union army and conspiring to dig up his fortune and spirit it away. In a fit of insane rage, Lipscomb loaded a pistol and killed the unfortunate slave with one shot to the head.

Lipscomb's wife was alternately concerned for and in fear of her husband. On several occasions he accused her of plotting to steal his gold and silver and threatened to kill her. His children grew frightened of him and fled at his approach. Soon the disturbed farmer was unable to sleep at night, preferring to sit up in his favorite chair, cradling a gun in his lap and babbling about his treasure.

Early one morning, Lipscomb's wife crept cautiously down the stairs to check on her husband. An ominous quiet reigned throughout the house, and he was nowhere to be seen. She was undertaking a search of the upstairs rooms when she heard a piercing scream coming from the front yard. Looking out the second-story window, she saw her housekeeper cowering in fright near the well and pointing to something on the front porch. Hurrying outside, Mrs. Lipscomb found her husband's body hanging from a porch rafter. The deranged miser had committed suicide.

With the deaths of Sledge and Lipscomb, there was no one left alive who knew the location of the buried caches of gold and silver coins. Lipscomb had told his wife about the lead plate he'd buried near the well in the front yard but had not provided any details on the exact location. With the help of her slaves, Mrs. Lipscomb supervised the excavation of dozens of holes near the house, but nothing was ever found.

As the Civil War raged on, it became clear to Mrs. Lipscomb that she would soon lose the farm and property. Not wishing to delay any longer, she and her children packed their belongings into a wagon and fled to

Texas to live with relatives. The plantation was abruptly abandoned, and no one in La Grange ever heard from Lipscomb and her children again.

Almost one hundred years after the end of the Civil War, a resident of the nearby town of Franklin, Georgia, named Titus Johnson was exploring around the ruins of the old Lipscomb plantation. As he stood near the long-abandoned well, he caught a glimpse of an object protruding from the ground several paces away. It appeared to be the edge of a platter. Curious, Johnson dug it up and beheld the strange artifact. It was a lead plate, but on one side a gold coin had been crudely hammered into it, and on the opposite side a silver coin was similarly embedded. Completely unaware of the significance of his discovery, Johnson carried the plate home with him and placed it on a shelf in his garage.

One week later, Johnson retrieved the plate with the intention of removing the old coins and trying to find out if they were worth anything. As he pried one coin from the plate, he noticed some numbers and arrows that had been scratched onto the surface. Taking a brush, he cleaned the dirt from the plate and found Lipscomb's directions to one of his buried treasures. After cleaning the opposite side, he found more of the same.

Excited by his find, Johnson carried the plate back to the Lipscomb plantation and stood at the site where he had unearthed it. After replacing the plate in the shallow hole, it became clear to Johnson that the directions inscribed on the surfaces were useful only when the plate was lying in the precise position and alignment originally determined by the plantation owner. Unless the plate was oriented exactly as he found it, the directions were useless. Because he could not remember the exact position of the plate, Johnson was never able to locate the treasure.

Today, even the location of Lipscomb's old well is unknown. Johnson eventually returned the lead plate to the shelf in his garage, and when he passed away in 1981 his belongings were distributed among his relatives. No one knows what became of the lead plate bearing the directions to the lost treasure.

The front yard of Lipscomb's old plantation house has been searched many times over the past hundred years, and portions of it have been excavated. The two caches of gold and silver coins, worth an immense fortune today, have never been found.

CHAPTER ELEVEN

Buried Weapons at
Cross Hollows, Arkansas

CROSS HOLLOWS, ARKANSAS, WAS A TINY OZARK SETTLEMENT LOCATED in a narrow valley ten miles east-northeast of Fayetteville. In 1861, the community was only twenty years old and composed of just a few small farms and a sawmill. In November of that year, Confederate general Ben McCulloch led an army of twelve thousand soldiers into the town. Here, they intended to establish a winter headquarters that would serve as an arms and ammunition depot for the war effort in that region of the country.

Several wooden barracks were erected in two long rows that stretched one mile along the valley. Over a period of time, weapons and munitions were delivered to this location and stored in a number of wood-frame buildings that had been constructed for that purpose. In addition to rifles and pistols, a number of cannons were also stored at the Cross Hollows location.

Early one morning, McCulloch received a scouting report that a large contingent of Union troops under the command of Major General Samuel R. Curtis was approaching the valley. A quick assessment by McCulloch determined that he did not have the manpower to withstand an assault by such an immense force. Acting with haste, McCulloch gave orders to his men to conceal the arms, destroy all the buildings, and abandon the area.

General Ben McCulloch
PEE WEE KOLB

As soldiers removed rifles, pistols, ammunition, and canons, they were followed by a detachment that set fire to the buildings. All the war materials were loaded into wagons or strapped onto mules and carried to the top of an adjacent ridge. Here, a long trench was excavated and the weapons and related gear dumped in. The trench was quickly covered over, and the soldiers fled the valley.

Several hours later, when Curtis and his army arrived in Cross Hollows, all they found were burned buildings and the scattered remnants of the Confederate camp. Though they searched throughout the valley, they found no sign of arms and assumed the Rebel soldiers carried everything away with them as they retreated toward the south. It never occurred to Curtis to search the nearby ridges.

During the closing months of the Civil War, several of the surviving Confederate soldiers who were involved in the caching of the arms and ammunition supply atop the ridge at Cross Hollows related the tale to others. A number of the soldiers indicated that, once they were discharged from the army, they intended to return to the area and attempt to retrieve some of the rifles. As far as is known, none ever did. By the time the war was over, the soldiers had returned to their homes and farms to set about getting things back in order. They either lost interest in the cache or could not remember exactly where it was located.

Today Cross Hollows is a ghost town. None of the original buildings remain, and there is little to suggest that the site was once home to over one thousand Confederate soldiers. Somewhere atop one of the nearby ridges that border the valley, hundreds of Confederate rifles and pistols, along with several canons, still lie buried. It is estimated that the antique weapons in this cache would fetch handsome prices.

Chapter Twelve

Callahan Mountain Treasure

Between the towns of Springdale and Rogers in Benton County in northwestern Arkansas, an impressive limestone formation, Callahan Mountain, has served as a landmark for many years. Many of the people living near Callahan Mountain are descendants of pioneers who settled in the area during the year prior to the Civil War. The following story has been attributed to several old-timers who recalled hearing it from their parents and grandparents.

At one point during the War between the States, a ragged and rather depleted company of thirty-five Confederate soldiers was fleeing a regiment of Union troops in northwestern Arkansas. The pursuit had lasted for days. The Rebels were weak from hunger, having run out of supplies two days earlier. Their horses, which were already exhausted from a long march the previous week, were tiring and refusing to continue. A gelding had already dropped dead in its tracks. Since the mounts were useless, fleeing Rebels abandoned them within a mile of Callahan Mountain.

Securing what gear they could carry, the soldiers hiked toward the mountain, hoping to find a suitable defensive position at or near the top. With difficulty, they ascended the slope. At the summit, they dug trenches and stacked rocks to form a low parapet. When they finished, they felt confident they would be able to defend themselves against the Yankees should the enemy choose to attack.

A half-day later, one of the Confederate scouts spotted the Union soldiers ascending the slopes and approaching their position. He reported to the exhausted company that the enemy was still several hours away. He also informed them that the Yankees outnumbered them by a considerable margin and were better armed.

As the Union soldiers neared the top of the mountain, the Rebel soldiers elected to excavate a hole and hide their valuables so that the Yankees would not come into possession of them should they prevail. They quickly dug a shallow hole into which they deposited coins, currency, watches, rings, and anything else of value. After refilling the hole, they rolled a huge rock into position on top of it. Years later, one of the surviving Confederate soldiers said it took twenty-one men to move the rock.

A short time later, the Yankees arrived and the battle was on. The exchange of gunfire lasted for two hours, enough time for the Rebels to decide that continuing the fight was folly bordering on suicide. As the sun began to set, there ensued a lull in the battle, and the Confederate soldiers decided to sneak away under cover of darkness. Crawling from the hastily erected breastwork, they crept over to the western edge of the mountain and descended the slope. They agreed to return as a unit to Callahan Mountain and retrieve their valuables at the first opportunity.

A few days later, these same soldiers found themselves involved in the famous battle of Pea Ridge, which was fought not far from Callahan Mountain. Every member of the Rebel company was killed. On one was found a journal that detailed the caching of the valuables atop Callahan Mountain.

To this day, the cache of Civil War–era valuables remains hidden atop Callahan Mountain under a large rock that would take a score of men to move.

CHAPTER THIRTEEN

The Alonzus Hall Treasure

ALONZUS HALL WAS ONE OF SEVERAL NOTORIOUS OUTLAWS WHO, WITH his gang, roamed the Ozark Mountains during the Civil War, robbing and murdering settlers and travelers. Hall has been described as a handsome young man, tall, with deep-set blue eyes and a charming, disarming smile. A charismatic individual, he had no trouble making friends, and in every settlement he visited he became a favorite of the ladies. His confident demeanor and self-possession made it easy for him to assemble a band of followers to help him perpetrate his criminal ways throughout the region.

In addition to being clever and crafty, Hall had a strong sense of adventure and appeared to thrive on danger. The combination of his high-spirited nature and mercenary bent inspired him and his gang to attempt a number of daring holdups.

One such spate of venturesome criminal activity led to Hall's undoing and eventually cost him his life. Before he died, however, Hall admitted to burying a fortune in gold coins, a cache that apparently still lies concealed today in a small cave beneath the waters of Table Rock Lake near the Missouri–Arkansas border.

Alonzus Hall and his gang were well known throughout the Ozarks, and it was unlikely any other outlaw was feared more. The Hall gang ranged from just north of Springfield, Missouri, southward into Arkansas. Because law enforcement was unsophisticated to nonexistent in this wild land, the bandits raided and pillaged at will, spreading terror throughout the ridges and valleys.

During the early part of April 1862, the Hall gang was particularly active. The outlaw leader led his band of six cutthroats into the settlement of Centralia, Missouri, and at gunpoint robbed the bank of $62,000 in gold coins. After fleeing the town, the outlaws rode south into the rugged Ozarks. The Centralia townsfolk, ill-equipped to pursue well-armed and dangerous men into wild, isolated regions of the mountain range, were reluctant to organize a posse. The gang was sure to know every trail and hiding place; the citizens were unfamiliar with the territory.

As the outlaws rode south, they stopped at two small farmsteads. After requesting and receiving food for themselves and grain for their horses, they robbed each of the farmers. At one farm they took $4,000 and at the other $6,000, all in gold coins. Following this, they rode deeper into the range.

Union army captain W. F. McCullough was in command of a company of soldiers temporarily encamped near the Frisco Railroad tracks twenty-five miles west of Springfield. Here, he received word of the Centralia bank robbery. As it turned out, the captain and his soldiers had been pursuing the Hall gang for several months. Within hours of the robbery, he received orders to undertake a search for them and attempt to capture them at any cost.

The day after learning of the bank robbery, McCullough received word that the outlaws had been seen traveling south along the old Wilderness Road and were last spotted in Greene County, Missouri. He ordered his men to break camp, mount up, and pursue the bandits at once. With McCullough in the lead, the soldiers rode twelve hours straight with scarcely a break. At that pace, McCullough planned to overtake the gang within the next day or two.

The trail led the soldiers through Greene County, into Christian County, and then into Stone County and the White River. During the second day of tracking, one of the army scouts reported to McCullough that he had spotted the outlaws camped under a ledge near the bank of the White River about one mile away. The captain ordered his men forward and told them to prepare to engage the bandits.

Aware of the possibility of pursuit, Hall had posted lookouts along the trail to the campsite. One of them spotted the approaching soldiers and immediately alerted the rest of the gang.

On receiving news of the soldiers, Hall and one of his henchmen gathered up all the gold coins and carried them to a nearby cave. They divided the loot into four equal piles and then stuffed each pile into a buckskin bag. The two men scraped out a shallow trench into which they placed the sacks. After filling the hole, they covered it with rocks and debris, making it appear just like the rest of the cave floor.

By the time they finished hiding the gold coins, Hall and his companion could hear gunfire coming from the campsite and assumed the soldiers had arrived. The two men raced back to the campsite to join in the fight.

McCullough had launched a vicious attack on the outlaws, who were heavily outnumbered and outgunned. The fighting was brief, lasting only about five minutes. By the time it was over, three of the Union soldiers and six of the outlaws were dead. Alonzus Hall had been shot through the stomach. When the soldiers found him, they at first thought he was dead, but one of them noticed the shallow breathing of the wounded man and summoned McCullough.

The captain saw to it that Hall's wound was bandaged. Following this, he was loaded into a wagon and transported to a temporary bivouac area along the White River near the present-day town of Reeds Spring. Throughout the night, Hall suffered terribly, and the next morning he was taken to the Union army general hospital at Springfield.

The army surgeon summoned to treat Hall's wound was a man named Dr. Boucher. Following an examination, Boucher concluded that a musket ball had done irreparable damage as a result of penetrating the outlaw's lower intestines. Boucher rebandaged him, administered some morphine, and reported to McCullough that he did not think his patient would live more than another day or two.

A few hours later, Boucher returned to Hall's bedside. He reexamined the wound and checked the outlaw's vital signs. A few hours later, Hall regained consciousness, looked around, and spotted the physician. Boucher, noting Hall was awake, approached and informed him of his condition.

The following morning, Hall, feeling somewhat invigorated, summoned the doctor to his bedside. When Boucher arrived, Hall told him he wanted to make a confession. Since McCullough had departed on another mission, Boucher was the ranking officer in the camp. As such, he consented to take Hall's statement. Securing a hospital journal and a pen, he scribbled copious notes as the gang leader related the story of the recent robbery and the flight into the mountains.

Hall told Boucher all that had transpired from the time of the Centralia bank robbery until the attack by Union troops at the campsite on the White River. He stated that the $62,000 from the bank, along with the gold coins he stole from the two farmers, was buried in a cave near the old ferryboat crossing where the Wilderness Road met the White River. As he spoke, Hall expressed regret at taking the money from the farmers. He asked Boucher to retrieve the cache and make certain the money was returned to the two men. As Hall spoke, Boucher took detailed notes, filling several pages of a journal. The following morning, when he went to check on Hall's condition, the outlaw was dead.

Dr. Boucher was confused about what to do with Hall's information. His military responsibilities required that he file a report with his superiors, the sooner the better. But the physician was tempted by the potential of great wealth in the form of gold coins lying buried in a shallow hole in a cave less than a day's ride from the hospital. Boucher wrestled with the decision for only a few minutes before giving in to the temptation of riches.

The physician hid the journal. Because he was committed to his military obligation for at least two more years, he decided to bide his time, expecting that on his discharge he would travel to the intersection of the Wilderness Road and the White River to retrieve the gold.

Unexpectedly, Boucher was transferred to a more active military post in the east. He hid the journal among some files at the hospital in Springfield, hoping someday to return for it.

There exists no record that Dr. Boucher ever returned to Springfield. Years later, while moving out of the Springfield hospital, an employee discovered the old journal containing Boucher's notes on Hall's confession. He turned it over to hospital administrators.

By the time the first decade of the twentieth century rolled around, several people had had access to the contents of the journal. The descriptions of the bank robbery and the subsequent flight through the Ozark Mountains were quite vivid. Equally detailed was the account of the attack by the Union forces on the outlaw camp and the burying of a total of $72,000 in gold coins and other money in the small cave.

The journal contained a complete description of the cave in which the money had been cached. Hall had told Boucher that the cave was not far from the overhanging ledge where the soldiers attacked the outlaw camp. Once the loot was buried, it took only a few short minutes until Hall and his companion returned to the fray.

The cave was described as being slightly illuminated as a result of a shaft of sunshine beaming through a narrow crack in the limestone ceiling. The two men buried the booty in the cave floor at the approximate center of the pool of light.

It is a simple task to locate the point at which the old Wilderness Road intersects with the White River. It is apparent on several maps of the region. It would likewise seem an easy task to locate the overhanging ledge as well as any small nearby caves. The overriding problem in the search for Alonzus Hall's lost treasure, however, lies in the fact that the waters of Table Rock Lake have inundated the site.

Close to where the treasure is believed to be buried is the Kimberling Bridge. Some suggest that the construction of the bridge may have obliterated any traces of the submerged overhang and the cave. Others insist that the site likely remains intact but lies under several feet of water.

There is no evidence that the Alonzus Hall treasure was ever recovered. The consensus among professional treasure hunters is that the money still lies buried in a small cave that may only be accessed via a scuba diving expedition.

CHAPTER FOURTEEN

Lost Cherokee Gold

DURING THE CIVIL WAR, PARTS OF INDIAN TERRITORY (NOW OKLAhoma) had been occupied by both Union and Confederate armies. Though no major battles were ever fought here, aspects of the war did inflict elements of tragedy on many area residents. One such tragedy resulted in the caching of a small fortune in gold that has never been found to this day.

For the most part, the Indian tribes that lived in the territory remained neutral during the conflict. Few of them had any interest in the philosophical differences between Northern and Southern white men, and life was difficult enough just trying to make a living on the new lands on which the tribes were forced to settle. The only advantage the Indians could see to having troops in the area was related to the fact that they provided some element of protection against the roving bands of outlaws that preyed on isolated communities and farms. Once the troops withdrew, however, many of the bandit gangs saw increased opportunities to reenter the area and renew depredations.

A Cherokee Indian named Usray lived with his son, daughter-in-law, and their young child in the wooded foothills of the Ozark Mountains just east of the town of Sallisaw in the eastern part of the territory near the Arkansas border. Usray had been granted a parcel of land on which he raised some crops along with a few cattle and hogs to sustain the family. In addition, Usray was well known locally for the fine horses he raised. Anyone in the area who had need of a sturdy work animal, a decent riding mount, or even a blooded racing horse would seek out Usray.

When Union soldiers occupied the area, they occasionally found it necessary to replenish their supply of mounts. In a short time, they learned that the best horses to be found in the hills belonged to Usray. On several occasions, the Yankee soldiers visited the Usray farm to purchase riding mounts and pack animals. They always paid in gold coins.

A frugal man content to live on his farm, Usray had little need of money. He always placed the gold coins in a tin box that he kept hidden in the crawl space under the wooden floor in his small cabin. One day, he intended to turn it all over to his son.

As the end of the war approached, the soldiers gradually pulled out. Initially, Usray regretted the departure of the troops and the loss of the opportunity to do business with them. Otherwise, he was happy to see them leave. Happy, that is, until the outlaws began moving back into the region. Concerned that desperadoes might arrive at his farm now that there was no military protection, Usray pastured his best stock in a concealed meadow several hundred yards away from the cabin, hoping the animals would escape the notice of roving horse thieves.

Usray was also concerned about the cache of gold coins under the floor of his cabin. One day he removed the tin box containing the coins. To the box he added his wife's jewelry and a gold watch he had owned for many years. He wrapped the box in an old sheepskin rug and told his grandson he was going to bury it out in the woods where no one would ever find it.

Usray, accompanied by his grandson, walked the short distance from the cabin to the spring from which the family drew water. Telling the child to wait there, the old man disappeared into the nearby hills. After returning to the spring half an hour later, Usray told the boy he'd buried the box of gold and jewels in a secret location.

That evening as they sat down to dinner, they heard riders approach and call out. Fearing the newcomers might be outlaws, Usray instructed his family to hide in the crawl space under the floor. Once they were out of sight, the old man walked out onto the porch in response to the call.

Four men sat on horseback just beyond the small stoop. They were a ragged-looking lot and could be mistaken for nothing other than outlaws. The leader, a man with a scarred face and unkempt hair that spilled out from under a wide-brimmed felt hat, wore several pistols and a large knife tucked in his belt. He spurred his horse a few steps toward the porch and addressed Usray. He said he had learned of the recent gold payment the Union army made to him for horses and demanded that it be turned over immediately. As he spoke to the Indian, he gestured with a rifle he carried in his hand.

Calmly, Usray answered that he had earned that money and needed it for his family. He explained he was not about to turn it over to worthless men too lazy to work for a living. Enraged, the leader asked for the money once again, warning the old man that if he did not turn it over he would be killed. In response, Usray stood squarely on the porch and folded his arms across his chest in a gesture of defiance. Unafraid, he held the gaze of the outlaw.

At a signal from the leader, a member of the group rode forward, uncoiled a rope, and tossed a loop over the head of the Indian. Turning his horse and spurring it, he pulled Usray off the porch and into the dirt. After tying the end of the rope to the saddle horn, the rider dragged Usray across the clearing and into the edge of the woods near the spring. The other riders approached, dismounted, and pulled the Indian to his feet, asking him once again to turn over the gold, telling him they were going to hang him if he refused.

The rider untied the rope from the saddle horn and tossed it over a low-hanging tree limb. Together, the four outlaws pulled the old man into the air and let him dangle there for a moment before letting him drop to the ground. Dazed, Usray choked and gagged as he tried to draw air into this lungs. At the same time, the grandson crawled out of the hiding place under the floor and watched in horror as the outlaws tortured his grandfather.

Thrice more the raiders raised Usray off the ground with the rope. When they allowed him to drop to the ground, they beat him as he gasped for breath. Still, the old man refused to reveal the location of the gold.

One of the outlaws removed Usray's moccasins and threatened to pull out his toenails. In response, the Indian spit into the face of his tormentor. Angered, the outlaw carried out his threat, but Usray bore the pain stoically, refusing to provide the men the satisfaction of watching him suffer.

Frustrated, and wearying of the effort of trying to get the old man to reveal the location of the gold, the leader of the gang stabbed Usray in the chest and ordered his henchmen to hang him. Following this, they turned their attention toward the cabin.

Ignoring the sobbing grandson, they turned over furniture and ransacked the small cabin until they were certain the gold was not there. The frightened son and his wife went undiscovered beneath the floor. Finally, finding nothing of value, the outlaws rode away.

The grandson informed his mother and father when the killers had departed, and they came out from hiding. The boy told them what he had seen the men do to his grandfather. They went to the spring, cut the old man down, and cried over his body.

The next morning they dug a grave and buried him. Following the funeral, the boy told his parents about Usray taking the gold into the hills and burying it at some secret location so outlaws could not get it.

While Usray had no need for the gold coins and jewelry, he died protecting his wealth so that his son and his family could have it. Unfortunately, the Indian died before he was able to reveal the location to anyone. Several attempts were made to locate the secret cache, but history does not report that it was ever found.

There is a record of the location of the Usray homestead. A short distance from the old cabin can be found a spring. It is likely that from the spring a trail winds into the adjacent hills, a trail followed by Usray when he sought a place to hide his gold coins. A fifteen-minute hike up this trail might place a searcher in close proximity to the Cherokee Indian's lost treasure cache.

CHAPTER FIFTEEN

The Incredible Journey of the Confederate Treasury

THE END OF THE CONFEDERATE STATES OF AMERICA OCCURRED DURING the spring of 1865. The South had suffered staggering defeats, leadership was in disarray, and the treasury did not contain enough money to continue to support the war effort. The last official meeting of the leaders of the would-be nation was held in April at Abbeville, South Carolina, as President Jefferson Davis and his cabinet fled approaching Union forces.

The Confederate treasury, though depleted, was still a significant store of gold and silver coinage. Among the items debated by the Southern leaders was the fate of what remained of this money. Some researchers believe the decision makers decided to move the store of wealth in order to protect it from the Northern invaders. Others of a more cynical nature expressed confidence in the notion that the leaders wanted the gold and silver transported someplace where they might more easily get their hands on it following the Yankee victory.

When General Robert E. Lee told President Davis that General Ulysses Grant's forces had penetrated the Confederate lines at Petersburg and that Richmond was about to be taken, Davis ordered an evacuation of the region. In the process, he gave Captain William H. Parker the responsibility of moving the treasure to a new location.

Parker was an officer in the Confederate Navy with a stellar record. He took his new assignment seriously. On the afternoon of April 2, 1865, Parker, enlisting the help of sixty midshipmen from a training vessel anchored on the James River, loaded the entire wealth of the Confederate treasury into a boxcar. This was to be the first of many transfers to take place over the next few days. Around midnight, the train departed Richmond bearing, according to most experts, an estimated $1 million. Others claim reports as high as $30 million, but there exists little evidence to support such claims.

By the time the train reached Danville, Parker received additional orders to move the treasure on to Charlotte, North Carolina, and store it in the abandoned United States Mint located there. No sooner was this done than Parker learned General George Stoneman's cavalry was headed in that direction and that the general might be interested in the treasure.

Parker ordered the treasure removed from the mint; packed into barrels with sacks of coffee, flour, and sugar; and reloaded onto the train. No sooner had this been accomplished than Parker was provided information that the railroad was out of service beyond Charlotte. He hurriedly transferred the containers from the train onto wagons.

While in the process of loading the treasure, Parker learned that Varina Davis, the wife of the Confederate president, was living in Charlotte with her children. Parker located her and persuaded her to travel south with him under military escort before the Union soldiers arrived.

On April 16, Parker's detachment arrived at Newberry, South Carolina. The trains were running, so the captain had the treasure-filled barrels and sacks loaded into another boxcar and then continued toward Abbeville.

When the detachment reached Abbeville, Mrs. Davis decided to leave the train and remain with some friends who lived nearby. While Mrs. Davis seemed unconcerned, Parker was ill at ease with the arrangement. Convinced, however, that the Union cavalry was in pursuit of him and the treasure, he felt it necessary to abandon the area immediately. He decided to travel on to Washington, Georgia, a few miles across the Savannah River to the southwest. Since the train did not go in that direction, Parker once again had the treasure removed from the boxcar and loaded onto wagons. After bidding farewell to Mrs. Davis, he crossed the river into Georgia.

This part of Georgia had not suffered as much from Union raiding as had the rest of the state. Parker was confident he could locate a sizeable military unit here that could take over the responsibility for the gold and silver he was transporting. The captain was growing anxious to be rid of the burden of the entire wealth of the Confederate nation.

On arriving at Washington, Parker learned that a command of some two hundred Confederate soldiers was holding Augusta fifty miles to the southeast. Running low on certain provisions, Parker traded flour and coffee to Washington residents for eggs, milk, and chickens. He then had his men load the treasure once more in a railroad car. Then, he ordered the train to Augusta.

At Augusta, the frustrated Parker discovered that it was not as easy to reassign the treasure as he had hoped. The officers there informed him that the war was over and that they were merely awaiting the arrival of the Union troops to arrange for an orderly surrender of the town, receive their pay, and go home. Possession of the Confederate treasury, they explained to him, would complicate matters, and they wanted nothing to do with it. One of the leaders even advised Parker to return the treasure to the now civilian leaders of the Confederate government who, at that very moment, were fleeing from Union soldiers across the Savannah River into Georgia. Among those in flight was Jefferson Davis himself.

Mistakenly, Parker decided Abbeville would be the likeliest place to locate Davis so he could ask him what to do with the treasure. He was convinced that Davis knew his wife was there and would try to find her. The fastest route to Abbeville was back through Washington, so Parker ordered the train to return. There, the now monotonous task of transferring the gold and silver back into wagons was once again completed and the journey to Abbeville was underway.

Less than one hour out of Washington, Parker, much to his surprise and chagrin, encountered Mrs. Davis and her children fleeing Abbeville with a small cavalry escort. She informed Parker that she had not seen her husband and had no idea where he might be.

On April 28, Parker and his command finally arrived at Abbeville, unloaded the wealth from the wagons, stored it in an empty warehouse just outside of town, and placed a heavy guard around it. That evening as

Jefferson Davis
PEE WEE KOLB

he was dining, Parker received word from one of his scouts that a large contingent of Union forces was a few miles north of the town and would arrive soon. Panicked, Parker ordered his men to reload the treasure onto a railroad car. He then ordered the engineer to prepare to depart, but before the train could be started, several hundred soldiers appeared at the north end of the town, all riding straight toward the train.

Fortunately for the harried Parker, the soldiers turned out to be a Confederate company escorting President Davis and what was left of his cabinet. Parker met with Davis and related his misadventures with the treasury. To his great relief, Davis ordered the responsibility for the gold and silver be transferred to the acting secretary of the Treasury, John H. Reagan. Almost as quickly, Reagan shifted the responsibility to John C. Breckenridge, the secretary of war. Breckenridge, not thrilled with this new and heavy burden, passed it on to General Basil Duke. Duke did not care for the responsibility either, but he had no one to pass it on to. Duke assumed the assignment with his customary dignity and rigid military bearing.

Duke was one of the few remaining Confederate generals, and his command was a motley assortment of nearly one thousand poorly armed and equipped volunteers who wanted nothing more than to go home. They were deserting in droves. Once the soldiers learned the war was over, several at a time would slip away and return to their farms and homes throughout the now devastated South.

Close to midnight on May 2, General Duke urgently ordered the gold and silver transferred once again from the boxcar to wagons. Duke had learned earlier in the evening that Union patrols were thick in the area and felt he would be lucky to be able to transport the gold and silver farther south and away from the advancing Yankees. Duke believed that Union officials were now aware that the treasure was in the area and would attempt to seize it. With his remaining force of troops, Duke moved the treasure out of Abbeville during the dark of night. Jefferson Davis and his remaining cabinet, grateful for the escort, rode along. Several of the troops stayed far to the rear of the column keeping an eye out for pursuit, and a dozen more rode along the flanks, prepared to ward off an attack by Yankees.

During a rest stop around midmorning of the following day, Duke promised his soldiers that when they reached Washington they would be paid in gold coins from the treasury they were escorting. Knowing the war was over and anxious to be on their way, the troops clamored for payment on the spot. The soldiers were also concerned that Union troops might suddenly appear and seize the money before they could get what they were due. For the rest of the day, Duke and a paymaster counted out thirty-two dollars for each soldier in the command.

This done, the wagons were escorted across the Savannah River toward Washington, Georgia. Every few minutes, Duke received word from scouts that the Yankee soldiers were only minutes away from attacking his column. At the first opportunity, the general ordered his command to leave the trail and take refuge in a large farmhouse belonging to a man named Moss. The barrels and sacks of gold and silver were unloaded from the wagons and stacked in the farmhouse kitchen. Duke then stationed his men at strategic points around the farmhouse and told them to prepare for a Yankee attack on the traveling treasury. The attack never materialized.

The Confederates spent the night at the farm. Very few were able to sleep since they were anticipating trouble at any moment. When scouts reported the next morning that no Yankees were in sight, Duke ordered the gold and silver loaded back onto the wagons. It was carried into Washington without incident.

At Washington, Duke turned the treasury over to Captain Micajah Clark. Earlier that day, Jefferson Davis, in his last official duty as president of the Confederacy, appointed Clark as the official treasurer of the Confederate States of America. Following this, Davis, along with his wife and children, fled deeper into the South. They were captured six days later.

Treasurer Clark decided that his first obligation in his new position was to count the money. According to the Treasury record, the exact amount was $288,000.90. It was, in truth, considerably less than what Parker had left Richmond with. Through the succeeding years, there has been a great deal of speculation as to what happened to the rest of the money. Thirty years later, Parker wrote an account of his adventures with the treasury and suggested that Captain Clark may have submitted a false accounting of what was turned over to him and kept the difference.

A significant number of researchers are convinced that Jefferson Davis himself appropriated much of the wealth before turning it over to Clark and then fled with it. They further speculated that Davis had buried portions of it at several different locations along the road before being apprehended. In any event, Clark paid off a few more of the soldiers out of the remaining funds and had the rest packed into kegs and wooden boxes.

On May 14, two officials representing a Virginia bank arrived in Washington with a Federal order for the total amount of the treasury.

The bank apparently held a claim on the wealth, and the two men were commissioned to secure it and return it to Richmond.

Following the military order to the letter, Clark turned what remained of the treasury over to the two bank representatives who, in turn, loaded it onto wagons and, under the protection of a military escort of some forty soldiers, departed for Richmond.

Most of the soldiers in the escort were young. And very few had seen any action during the war. For that reason, the two bank representatives were nervous throughout the trip. Soon after the column left Washington, a scout reported that it was being followed by a gang of outlaws made up of discharged Rebel soldiers and local toughs. The soldiers comprising the escort were ordered to take extra precautions as the small wagon train lumbered toward the Savannah River.

Travel was slow, and on the afternoon of May 22 the party arrived at the front yard of the home of Reverend Dionysius Chennault, only twelve miles out of Washington. The wagons were pulled into a large horse corral and drawn into a tight defensive circle. The guard was doubled and posted about the corral that night while the rest of the command tried to sleep.

At midnight the outlaws struck. Firing only a few shots, they surprised the inexperienced Federal guards, who quickly surrendered. The guards were tied up, and the remaining soldiers, who awakened at the first sound of shooting, were held at gunpoint by a handful of the outlaws. The leaders of the gang smashed open the boxes and kegs containing the gold and silver coins and stuffed their saddlebags full of the booty. Thousands of dollars' worth of coins were spilled onto the ground as the rest of the greedy outlaws surged forward and filled their pockets. Finally, carrying all they could hold, the outlaws mounted up and rode away on horses barely able to carry the combined weight of riders and loot. One of Reverend Chennault's daughters estimated that well over $100,000 worth of gold and silver coin was recovered from the ground the following morning.

The outlaws rode northwest to the bank of the Savannah River. On learning that they were being pursued by both Confederate soldiers and local law enforcement personnel, they hastily dug a pit and buried all the wealth in a common cache. They intended to escape pursuit and return for it another time. They set up camp for the night, intending to depart in the morning, but a company of soldiers encountered the bandits at dawn and killed every one of them.

What today is estimated to be worth well over $1 million in Confederate gold and silver coins is still buried in the ground somewhere on the south bank of the Savannah River and just off the trail.

Members of the Chennault family gathered up the fortune in coins that had spilled onto the ground during the robbery. Placing the gold and silver into kitchen pots and wooden crates, they buried it in a shallow hole adjacent to a nearby tributary of the Savannah River. Though they waited for a significant amount of time, no representatives of either the Union nor Confederate governments ever returned to the Chennault farm to claim any of the treasure.

The reverend cautioned his family members not to dig up any of the treasure until such time as the passions of the war died down and it would be safe to do so. Researchers have determined that the Chennault cache was never retrieved and still lies buried somewhere on the old farm. Over the years, a number of people have arrived at the farm to undertake a search for this rich portion of the Confederate treasury, but with no success.

In recent years, state-of-the-art technology associated with metal detectors has improved to the point that a number of professional treasure hunters began developing plans to make additional attempts at recovering the Chennault farm treasure. They have been disappointed to learn, however, that the small tributary near where the gold and silver were cached has been inundated by the waters of Clarks Hill Lake. According to the U.S. Army Corps of Engineers, the Chennault portion of the Confederate treasure now lies beneath thirty feet of water.

CHAPTER SIXTEEN

The Lost Treasures of General John H. Morgan

FOR YEARS, GENERAL JOHN H. MORGAN WAS THE PRIDE OF THE CON-federate army. As an officer, his record of command, leadership, and bravery was noteworthy, and it was inevitable that he would someday be promoted to general. Morgan was in charge of several successful raids for the Army of the South, in the process seizing arms, mounts, and funds that were used to support the war effort. These added to Morgan's growing reputation as a military genius and encouraged influential politicians to regard him as a future contender for political office.

In every case, Morgan carried out his duties and responsibilities beyond expectations, always earning lavish praise from his peers. There was more to Morgan's character, however, than many were aware; the general had a dark side related to his desire for great wealth. While lower-ranking officers were often placed in charge of confiscating horses, weapons, and ammunition, Morgan himself controlled a rapidly growing fortune in gold, silver, and currency.

As the end of the war approached, Morgan's career declined as a result of some poor military decisions. The great store of wealth he had accumulated during his numerous raids was never entirely accounted for, and many believed he simply decided to keep it for himself. There is a supposition among researchers that Morgan buried his treasure at certain locations along roads and trails the Confederate forces traveled. It has been estimated that Morgan had, while commanding a Rebel battalion, accumulated over $1 million in gold and silver coins and bullion as well as currency that would be worth several million dollars at today's values.

As his fortune grew, Morgan had it packed into crates and kegs and lashed onto several stout horses that, under heavy guard, remained with his command. With each raid, with each sack of a town, and with each addition of money from county treasuries and local banks, the wealth grew larger and the packhorses more numerous.

It was also learned that Morgan extorted large sums of money from local businessmen and farmers who lived in and near towns he raided. Accompanied by a well-armed contingent of cavalry, Morgan would ride up to a business or farmhouse and demand money. If he was refused, he would threaten to burn the building or domicile to the ground.

When Morgan was questioned about the gold and silver he transported, he would reply that he intended to deliver it to the Confederate treasury. As he gathered more and more wealth, however, he appeared less inclined to part with it. The general seemed to take pride in his treasure-laden packhorses and often bragged to his peers about transporting the fortune along with his command during military campaigns.

As the Union forces steadily advanced during 1863 and as the Confederate forces weakened, Morgan suggested to General Bragg that several large cavalry raids in the North might divert pressure from the Rebel troops. At the same time, suggested Morgan, more money could be confiscated along the way—money, he explained to Bragg, that could be used to fund the Southern cause.

At first Bragg was hesitant, but at the same time he was growing concerned that the Confederacy was running out of money. He finally relented and allowed Morgan to lead a command to the North. He cautioned the officer, however, to keep his forces on the south side of the Ohio River. Morgan agreed but had no intention of following Bragg's orders.

With a command of 2,460 men, Morgan advanced from Tennessee into Kentucky on July 1, 1863. All along the route, his army raided, looted, and pillaged towns, farms, communities, and even travelers. It was said that Morgan even robbed the collection boxes at local churches. Using the excuse that these new funds would be used to aid the Confederate cause, Morgan and a few members of his staff always seemed

General John Morgan
PEE WEE KOLB

to spend a great deal of money on themselves. Morgan and his closest associates always dined well on fine meals and expensive wines and were attended to by servants.

During the campaign, Morgan's army struck Salem, Kentucky, raiding and looting like bandits. The cavalrymen were so intent on acquiring money and goods and destroying the town that they paid little attention to the orders of their commanding officers. There ensued fighting, killing, raping, burning, and drunkenness, and it soon became clear that Morgan was losing control of his command. Following the Salem raid, Morgan had trouble maintaining discipline.

During the raid, hundreds of rifles were confiscated along with thousands of dollars. The guns and ammunition were shipped south to

Confederate troops in Tennessee and Virginia. Morgan kept the money, adding it to his personal wealth.

On the warm, still morning of July 4, Morgan led his troops into Versailles, Kentucky. After attacking the town, Morgan personally led a raid on the county treasury and confiscated in excess of $5,000, which he pocketed.

Disobeying Bragg's orders, Morgan and his men crossed the Ohio River, swarming into the state of Ohio and pillaging the towns of Jasper and Piketon. As on previous raids, Morgan's undisciplined soldiers vented their fury on the towns, behaving more like a mob than trained cavalrymen.

The continued breakdown of discipline and vigilance was to bring tragedy to Morgan's army. On July 18, a portion of Morgan's command was intercepted, attacked, and captured by Federal forces. The general was left with only nine hundred men. Massive Union forces were now closing in on Morgan from several directions. Normally a brilliant tactician, Morgan ignored the warnings of his scouts about the impending attack. The only precaution he took was to add extra guards to his treasure-laden pack train.

On July 26, the Ninth Michigan Cavalry launched an attack on Morgan's army at Salineville, Ohio. Thirty Confederate soldiers were killed within the first few minutes of battle, fifty more were wounded, and two hundred were captured outright. Realizing a crushing defeat was inevitable, Morgan, along with several fellow officers and his heavily guarded pack train in tow, fled the battle scene. Once away from the action, they headed south toward the Ohio River. Slowed by the heavy and cumbersome load of gold and silver, Morgan and his men made their way through woods and across farms and fields. Hours later, they were captured near West Point, Ohio. When Morgan and his officers were taken prisoner, none of the treasure was in his possession. Clearly, it had been buried somewhere along the escape route.

Morgan and his fellow officers were incarcerated at the state penitentiary at Columbus. Morgan, however, had no intention of remaining imprisoned for long. Within days of being jailed, the general organized an escape plan. Using metal tableware for digging tools, he and his men worked around the clock, excavated a tunnel, and escaped four months later on the evening of November 26, 1863. Traveling at night, Morgan and his officers eluded pursuers and eventually reached the safety of the Confederate lines far to the south.

When word of his July capture got around, Morgan's prestige began to wane, and he was thereafter ignored by Confederate leaders. Desperate for commanders, however, Confederate leaders assigned Morgan to take charge of 2,500 cavalrymen for a raid into Kentucky.

Departing from a location in Pound Gap, Virginia, Morgan led his soldiers at a rapid pace for 150 miles before arriving at the small town of Mount Sterling, Kentucky, on the morning of June 8, 1864. Following a brief battle, the Rebels took the small town. Morgan, apparently learning nothing from his previous raids, turned his troops loose to sack the town. While his men were looting, burning, and drinking, Morgan organized and participated in robbing the Mount Sterling bank of $80,000.

On June 11, his scouts failed him. Morgan's cavalry entered the town of Cynthiana and encountered a large contingent of Federal forces that had gone undetected. Following a vicious fight, Morgan's troops eventually defeated the Union soldiers. As the town burned to the ground, the general confiscated money from the local businessmen. A number of Confederate troops had been killed, and Morgan's command dwindled to fewer than a thousand men.

Morgan led his victorious but severely battered force to a field just outside of Cynthiana and ordered a temporary camp set up in order to rest men and horses alike. Meanwhile, Morgan began planning new strategies for adding to his wealth.

The following morning, as the Rebel soldiers began to awaken and leave their tents and bedrolls in search of breakfast, five thousand Union cavalrymen swooped onto the field and fired into the confused mass. Caught unaware and unprepared, the Rebels fought half-heartedly. Within thirty minutes, dozens were killed and the remainder captured. During the short battle, Morgan and two enlisted men dug a shallow trench and buried all the currency, coin, and bullion taken during the plunder of Mount Sterling and Cynthiana. This done, Morgan and a handful of his officers mounted up and fled the scene of battle. After days of hard riding, they reached Abingdon, Virginia, on June 24.

The embarrassing defeat at the field outside of Cynthiana was the final nail in the coffin for Morgan's reputation and career as a military man. Now, he was completely ignored by Confederate leaders. A number of prominent generals called for his court-martial for looting and extortion. They also filed a request for an investigation into what had become of all the gold, silver, and cash he had acquired during his raids, none of which was ever turned over to the Confederate treasury. A formal request for the return of the $80,000 taken from the Mount Sterling bank was drafted and delivered to the beleaguered general.

It will never be known whether or not Morgan would have capitulated and returned any of his buried fortune. On September 14, 1864, Union soldiers raided Confederate headquarters at Greenville, South Carolina, and Morgan was killed.

If General Morgan left maps or directions to any of his buried Civil War loot, they have never been located. Well over $1 million in gold, silver, and currency in 1864 values is believed to have been cached in several places along routes that he traveled. The richest caches are certainly the ones made while he was fleeing from the battle at Salineville, Ohio, and the one buried in the field near Cynthiana, Kentucky.

A number of artifact collectors have recovered Civil War–related items from the old battle site in the field outside of Cynthiana, but to date, not a cent of the buried treasure has been recovered. If Morgan's route from Salineville to the point where he was captured by the Union army near West Point, Ohio, could be determined, it is possible a search for the secret cache of what must amount to several million dollars' worth of gold and silver in today's values could prove successful.

CHAPTER SEVENTEEN

Field of Gold and Silver Coins

TASSO, TENNESSEE, IS AN APPALACHIAN FOOTHILLS TOWN THAT LIES just outside the western boundary of the Cherokee National Forest and five miles northeast of Cleveland. Just south of Tasso and adjacent to the railroad track is a farm field, one that has been in use for over 150 years. Scattered across this field lie dozens, if not hundreds, of relics from the Civil War. Somewhere in this field also lies a fortune in gold and silver coins, the remains of a great explosion that disabled a Confederate train during the War between the States.

The Cherokee Indians who originally settled this region called their community Chatata, an Indian word for "clear water." Here they planted crops and raised horses. Their productive and well-cared-for farms were admired and coveted by white men who entered the region. When the Cherokee were removed during the early 1830s, white settlers lost no time moving in and taking over the already well-established farms. The new occupants retained the Cherokee name for the village, and Chatata soon evolved into a productive and prominent agricultural center in southeastern Tennessee. In 1858, a railroad was laid through the area, connecting Chatata with the larger towns of Cleveland and Chattanooga to the southwest and Knoxville to the northeast.

When the Civil War came to this region, Chatata residents went about their business of planting, tending, and harvesting corn and other crops and trying to live as normally as they could under the circumstances. They saw hundreds of soldiers—Union and Confederate alike—pass through and around the town, but for the most part the small community was spared the misery experienced by so many others during the violent and bloody conflict.

Both Union and Confederate forces employed the railroad line, and it was not uncommon to see a Yankee troop train pass through in the morning and a Rebel one in the afternoon. In the spring of 1864, Company C of the Confederate Army of Tennessee was camped just outside of Chatata. The company had been ordered to scout the area and gauge the strength of any Union forces it encountered. If it was possible, the company was to attack and kill or capture any Yankees they found.

One morning, the commanding officer of Company C, a young and somewhat inexperienced captain, received word that a Union troop train was approaching from the southwest. The train was said to be transporting two thousand soldiers, a supply of rifles and ammunition, and three canons. The captain decided to try to wreck the train and confiscate the weapons.

The officer also learned that a Confederate express was pursuing the Yankee train. The Rebel train consisted of a locomotive and five cars. Most of the cars carried men and horses, but the second car behind the locomotive was transporting a large payroll in gold and silver coins destined for a Rebel camp ten miles up the line near Charleston. The payroll car, according to reports, was also carrying guns, ammunition, sabers, and other military equipment. The two trains traveled close enough that gunfire was often exchanged, and at least one Yankee had been killed.

The Rebel captain summoned Private Isaac Griffith and ordered him to set an explosive charge that would be detonated by the Union train passing over it. Once the train was disabled, said the captain, mounted Rebel soldiers would swoop down onto the scene and kill or capture any surviving Yankees. To spare Chatata any damage, Private Griffith was to set the charge on the tracks several hundred yards south of the town.

Pressed for time, Private Griffith hurriedly attached the explosive to the railroad bed at the designated location. Satisfied with the placement, Griffith leaped onto his mount and sped away to rejoin the rest of his fellows who had gathered on horseback on a nearby low hill to await the train.

Moments later, the mounted Confederates heard the two trains approaching rapidly. They also heard gunfire emanating from both. As the Union locomotive came into view, a huge cheer erupted from the expectant Rebels as they anticipated an easy victory. The cheering, however, turned to horrified silence as the Union train passed over the charges without setting them off. As it roared away, the Confederate locomotive passed over the same spot, setting off the dynamite and generating a gigantic explosion that destroyed the engine and the two cars behind it. The rest of the train jumped the tracks.

When the smoke cleared, the stunned Rebels saw pieces of train, military equipment, and fellow soldiers, dead and dying, scattered several dozen yards on either side of the railroad tracks. The wooden crate in which the payroll was packed was blown to bits, and gold and silver coins were hurled across the countryside to be deposited in the field.

The screams and cries of the wounded and dying reached the ears of the mounted Rebels. As the company surged forth to try to aid their stricken comrades, they were suddenly set upon by a large Yankee force that charged out of the nearby woods. The Rebels, completely unprepared for the onslaught, fled for their lives, unmindful of the orders shouted by their frantic captain. Several Rebels were killed or wounded as they raced across the field, but most escaped into the woods. A few were taken prisoner. After routing the enemy, the Union soldiers, ignorant of the payroll, looked over the accident scene and abandoned the area.

Attracted by the sound of the explosion and the billow of dark smoke that rose from the wreckage, Chatata residents raced to the scene and provided what help they could to the surviving Confederate soldiers. The gold and silver coins lay unnoticed in the field.

With the passing of time, the accidental demolition of the Confederate train faded from the memories of Chatata residents, and the incident became only a minor footnote in the history of the region. After the Civil War, Chatata grew and prospered and became one of several pleasant and attractive communities in the scenic foothills on the western side of the Appalachian Mountains.

In 1905, the residents of Chatata changed the name of the town to Tasso, the surname of an Italian gentleman who often rode the train through the small town. When the train stopped there to let off and take on passengers, Mr. Tasso would stand on the rear deck of the caboose and sing opera to any who cared to listen. The townspeople often gathered in large crowds to hear him.

In 1970, the story of the destroyed Confederate train returned to the attention of area residents as a result of a remarkable discovery by a Tasso youth. On a hot afternoon, with the dense noise of locusts buzzing in the trees, sixteen-year-old Ben Casteel was playing along Chatata Creek where it runs parallel to the railroad tracks for several yards. He noticed something slightly out of place in the muddy bottom of the shallow stream and investigated. To his surprise, he withdrew a Confederate saber from the thick mud. Though rusted and dirty, the saber was in good condition. On closer examination, it was determined that the weapon had been part of a shipment of military goods carried by the blown-up train. The recovery of the saber revived the tale, and people were soon walking through the field searching for more relics. That's when they began finding a few gold and silver coins.

Since the discovery of the saber, many other Civil War relics have been located: mess kits, silverware, parts of boots, brass buttons, and belt buckles. Very few coins were found, however, and a researcher who has examined the site has advanced a theory about what probably happened to them. He also claims to know where to find the coins.

Gold and silver, he explained, are heavy metals. When coins such as these lie on soft and often muddy soil, like that found in the field near Tasso, they gradually sink below the surface. The area near the railroad tracks is flooded once or twice each year when the creek overflows from heavy rains. When the ground is saturated with water, the individual grains of soil separate easily. This allows any dense object, such as a coin, to penetrate and sink. The local flooding is also believed to have added at least two, and perhaps as much as four, feet of silt to the field during the past 150 years. Thus, according to the researcher, the individual gold and silver coins will likely be found between five and ten feet below the present surface.

Locating the coins would mean removing a considerable amount of topsoil, a suggestion not endorsed by local farmers. One enterprising treasure hunter has suggested a series of narrow trenches be dug one at a time near the explosion site. Using a backhoe, each trench would be excavated to a depth of ten feet and the unearthed soil carefully examined for coins. This done, the trench would be filled and another dug. The plan, says the treasure hunter, would cause minimum disruption to farming activities.

If a recovery operation could be agreed on by all interested parties, the method might indeed yield a bountiful harvest of gold and silver coins as well as an array of Confederate Civil War relics.

CHAPTER EIGHTEEN

Buried Union Army Payroll

IN THE SPRING OF 1902, THE TOWN OF ROGERSVILLE, TENNESSEE, SUR-
vived the worst storm to strike the area in more than a decade. High
winds had destroyed several homes and removed the shingles and
toppled the chimneys of others. Creeks overflowed from the increased
runoff, fields were flooded, and crops were ruined. Huge trees had blown
down, their broken and torn roots splayed out like so many spider legs.

Several days after the storm, three boys were hunting rabbits in the
woods not far from town. As they walked through the debris of the earlier storm, they encountered a deadfall. At the base of the tree where it
had been uprooted were several holes from which thick roots had been
pulled out of the ground. Hoping to find a rabbit, one of the boys thrust
his hand into one of the holes. His fingers touched pieces of cold metal.
Grabbing one of them, he withdrew it and was surprised to discover it
was a silver coin. Further investigation revealed the hole was filled with
similar coins, all U.S. silver dollars dated 1862.

The three boys enlarged the hole and found a metal cooking pot filled
with silver dollars. The pot had evidently been tipped over when the roots
were pulled from the ground, spilling some of the coins.

The youths filled their pockets and game bags with the coins and
went home, intending to keep the discovery a secret. Their parents soon
found out, however, and encouraged the boys to turn the money over
to the authorities and let them try to find the rightful owner. The silver
dollars had a total face value of $1,512.

At the time, it was not clear who owned the land on which the coins were found, and the subsequent investigation lasted for weeks. Meanwhile, several newspapers reported the discovery, and the news spread nationwide.

A short time later, a Tennessee resident named Bobby Venable received a letter postmarked from New York. The letter was from an elderly man who had read about the discovery. He told Venable that he had been a corporal in the Union army in Tennessee during the Civil War and explained how the silver coins came to be buried.

Sometime in 1864, stated the letter writer, he was promoted to corporal and assigned to a Union escort transporting a huge payroll in silver coins for four hundred troops stationed near the Tennessee–North Carolina border. The dollars were carried in canvas sacks. As the escort approached Big Creek near Rogersville, a company of Confederate soldiers attacked it.

Badly outnumbered, the Union escort retreated into the nearby woods, searching for a place to take cover and fight. Once inside the perimeter of trees, the officer in charge ordered his men to dismount and return fire. For several hours, firing behind tree trunks and fallen logs, the Yankees held off the attacking Rebels. However, as the Union soldiers fell one by one, the eventual outcome of the skirmish grew clear.

Not wanting the payroll to fall into enemy hands, the commanding officer enlisted one of his men to help him hide the coins. That man was the corporal who wrote to Venable thirty-eight years later.

The officer and the corporal unloaded the payroll sacks and other supplies from the mules and went from tree to tree, digging shallow holes. Into each, they placed two or three of the coin-filled canvas sacks and a few supply items until all of it was hidden. The corporal recalled that next to one particularly thick tree he had dug one hole large enough to hold a cooking pot. After placing the pot in the hole, he stuffed it with several sacks of coins and then refilled the excavation. Once the payroll and supplies were hidden, the officer told the corporal they would return to retrieve the caches should they survive the attack.

Minutes after returning to the fight, the officer took a bullet through the head and died. Only a handful of Union soldiers remained alive. The corporal turned and fled into the woods, far from the sounds of combat.

The corporal said he wandered for days, finding neither food nor water. Eventually he came to an isolated farm. Not knowing the political sympathies held by the farmer, the corporal took a chance and knocked on the front door of the farmhouse. The farmer and his wife took him in, fed him, and gave him a clean set of clothes. The corporal thanked the couple, continued his flight, and, having had his fill of war and not wishing to experience any more of it, eventually made it home to New York. Once there, he realized he could be brought to trial as a deserter, so he lived in hiding for many years.

In his letter, the corporal stated that he and the officer buried portions of the military payroll in at least a dozen different locations, always at the base of large trees they believed would be easy to relocate.

Venable shared the letter with two friends. After the passage of several weeks, he decided to make it public. As a result, hundreds of hopeful treasure hunters came to Rogersville, each convinced he would be the one to dig up at least a portion of the Union payroll. Before long, the forest near Big Creek was swarming with men with picks and shovels. Weeks later, when the crowds departed, the landscape was dotted with hundreds of excavations.

Near the original discovery made by the three boys, a few Civil War relics were found, no doubt remnants from the skirmish. These included bridle bits, tools, a stirrup, and several buttons from both Yankee and Rebel uniforms. None of the remaining payroll, however, was located.

More time passed, and the tide of treasure hunters ebbed to insignificant numbers. Rogersville gradually returned to normal. In spite of several attempts by Venable to contact the former Union corporal, no more was heard from him. Soon, the incident was forgotten.

Perhaps someday another storm will strike the area near Rogersville, blowing shingles from roofs and felling large trees in the forest. In this manner, perhaps another cache of silver coins might be discovered and the search for others renewed.

CHAPTER NINETEEN

The Bechtler Coins

BETWEEN 1831 AND 1840, A SMALL, PRIVATELY OWNED MINT OPERATED
in the remote area of Rutherfordton, Rutherford County, located in the
North Carolina Appalachians. The owners mined, processed, and coined
nearly $40 million worth of gold over a nine-year period. The coins, cast
into denominations of $1.00, $2.50, and $5.00, were in general circula-
tion throughout parts of North Carolina, South Carolina, and northern
Georgia. During the Civil War, these coins were preferred over all others
by the government of the Confederacy for doing business.

As coins minted by the United States became available, these locally
made specie were gradually withdrawn from the area economy. Hundreds
of these old coins are now in the possession of collectors, and many more,
perhaps millions of dollars' worth, may still be found in and around
Rutherford County. Also waiting to be found in the area is the gold mine
from which the ore used to manufacture the coins came.

Few are aware of it, but most of the gold mined in the United States
between 1790 and 1840 came from western North Carolina and parts of
South Carolina and Georgia. North Carolina supplied most of the gold
coined by the U.S. mint in Philadelphia during that same period. According to a 1948 U.S. Geological Survey report, there were around three
hundred gold-producing mines in North Carolina alone. Rutherfordton,
located some forty miles southeast of Asheville in the western part of the
state, was known as America's gold mining capitol during the early 1800s.

Although most of the gold used for minting U.S. coins came from
western North Carolina, U.S. money was, in fact, very scarce in that

region. Because of that, a few area residents made their own from locally mined gold. These maverick coins were in common use throughout the region and were generally accepted by all.

In 1830, a German immigrant named Christopher Bechtler and his son, August, arrived in the tiny community of Rutherfordton. In Europe, the Bechtlers had been metallurgists and jewelers, and they hoped to put their rare skills to use in the gold fields of North Carolina.

The Bechtlers found a promising outcrop of gold ore in Rutherford County not far from the town. They settled onto the property and soon discovered that the outcrop, a deposit of gold-bearing quartz, was far richer than originally suspected. As they mined the ore, the two men decided to open their own mint. They built a roller and a stamp press and began producing high-quality specie in denominations of $1.00, $2.50, and $5.00. Area residents soon came to prefer the Bechtler coins to the Federal ones for conducting business, and they began to be used almost exclusively throughout the region.

For a time, the Bechtlers considered selling their gold to the U.S. mint but preferred minting their own coins. Hauling the heavy ore from western North Carolina to eastern Pennsylvania was a long and arduous trip, and it used up time that could be better spent mining the gold. During this period, remote and seldom-traveled roads were often unsafe, and there was always the danger of being robbed by highwaymen. Selling the gold to a broker or middleman also reduced profit. Given these considerations, the Bechtlers decided the optimum way to conduct their business was to fashion their own gold into what became known as "Bechtler coins." In a few years, the two men became very wealthy.

For nine years the Bechtler mine and mint prospered. It has been estimated that more than $40 million worth of coins (at today's values) were manufactured. Most went into the area economy.

The Bechtler mint, however, was not destined to endure. In 1840, the U.S. government opened a mint in Charlotte, seventy-five miles to the east of Rutherfordton. With U.S.-minted specie now available in the region, the Bechtlers were pressured by the Federal government to cease their private enterprise. The men did not object; by that time they had already made a fortune. Many western North Carolinians, however, still insisted on using the Bechtler coins. Most area merchants had been using the Bechtler coins for years and preferred them to the U.S. variety.

During the Civil War, the Bechtler coins were preferred, even in demand, by the Confederate government. More than one historian has noted that Confederate purchasing contracts often specifically called for payment to be made in Bechtler gold rather than U.S.-issued coins or paper money. In fact, metallurgical analysis showed that the Bechtler coins had a higher gold content than did the U.S.-minted coins. In addition, they were more plentiful in the area and more acceptable to merchants and suppliers, who had become accustomed to using them.

As the Civil War raged, and even after North Carolina joined the Confederacy, the western section of the state was spared much of the violence that disrupted the rest of the South. Though most of the conflict occurred elsewhere, many families in and near the Carolina Appalachians buried large caches of Bechtler coins so they could not be confiscated by roving bands of Yankee soldiers or by the numerous gangs of bandits who terrorized the countryside.

Within months of closing down the family gold mine, Christopher Bechtler, along with a large trunk filled with his gold coins, disappeared. He was traveling by wagon to nearby Buncombe County to pay off a debt. He was last seen at the Parris Gap tollgate, where he paused for a short visit with the operator. A few days later, Bechtler's wagon was found overturned in a deep ravine three miles west of the gap. His two horses had been killed, and their carcasses lay near the ruined wagon. Bechtler and the trunk full of coins were never seen again.

A short time later, August Bechtler abandoned the North Carolina property and moved into Rutherfordton. There, he opened a shop that made jewelry, firearms, and occasionally, in response to local demand, a few coins. He used the original rollers and dies in the process. Beset with serious health problems, August passed away a few years later, leaving his fortune and his business to his closest living relative, a cousin who had come to live with the Bechtlers five years earlier. The cousin, also named Christopher, and sometimes referred to as Christopher Junior, ran the business for several years. He eventually closed it down and moved away, leaving no information about where he was bound.

Christopher Bechtler
PEE WEE KOLB

Over time, the Bechtler coins gradually disappeared from general circulation to be replaced by Federal specie. As the coins became part of the region's history, the Smithsonian Institution saw fit to create a display of them. Coin collectors found them to be valuable both intrinsically and as historical artifacts. Since the 1960s, researchers have discovered that a number of current Rutherfordton residents still possess many of the old coins, which were handed down in the families. One family boasted a collection of several hundred. Some of these collections of Bechtler coins have been estimated to be worth from several hundred thousand dollars to well over a million on today's collector market.

Bechtler coins still turn up from time to time. One longtime Rutherfordton resident reported finding hundreds of the coins in a secret hiding place in the concrete-lined chimney of an old house that Christopher Bechtler had lived in. The coins were picked out of a square, hollow cement chamber. It has also been suggested that millions of dollars' worth of the coins were hidden during the Civil War and were never retrieved, the caches still lying buried on old homesteads in the region.

Some of the minting equipment once used by the Bechtlers is still around. The rollers and the stamp press, both valuable artifacts, are in the possession of local residents. The original dies used in the manufacture of the coins served as doorstops for a Rutherfordton family for decades. When World War II broke out, the lady of the house donated them to the government during a scrap metal drive.

The location of the original Bechtler mine with its seemingly inexhaustible source of rich gold was known about for generations. When Christopher Bechtler closed it down in 1840, the vein was reported to be as rich and abundant as the day it was discovered. Many believe that his son, August, reopened the mine for a short period during the mid-1840s and then shut it down for good. Sometime during the first decade of the twentieth century, the old mine was classified as a hazard and was covered up and fenced off. More time passed, and Rutherfordton residents forgot about the mine and its location. The site was eventually designated for use as a sanitary landfill.

In 1945, a longtime Rutherfordton resident searched for the old mine and found it. He claimed he and his father removed the covering from the old shaft and lowered themselves into it by rope. Once inside the old excavation, they walked around and explored it. They found old tools, artifacts, furniture, and mining apparatus. The old-timer recalled that the air inside the shaft was bad and smelled strongly of gas. He also reported that the shaft was nearly knee-deep in water and that water was seeping into the mine from cracks in the shaft wall. He and his father climbed out after a half hour and never went back. To his knowledge, he said, no one else has ever been inside the old shaft.

Over the years, a few adventurous souls have drawn up plans to reopen the old Bechtler gold mine. While such a thing was possible a few years ago, it is not likely to happen today. The old gold mine is a victim of progress. Construction projects and real estate developments have turned the old site into commercial and residential use, completely cutting off access to the rich gold ore that lies below the surface.

Rutherfordton today is a pleasant community sprawling attractively in the shadows of the Carolina Appalachians. It is regarded as a typical small American town, and few residents and visitors that walk the streets and travel the roads in this village of some 3,500 souls are aware that it was once a place where a fortune in gold was mined and minted.

Chapter Twenty

Pots of Gold

As the Civil War began drawing to a close during the latter months of 1864, it was becoming painfully obvious to the leaders of the Confederate army that the South was losing. Several Southern generals, realizing the truth of the eventual outcome, began to express more interest in salvaging what was left of the Confederate treasury than winning battles. To that end, much of the Southern army's wealth, which was intended for the purchase of arms, ammunition, and riding stock, was hurriedly hidden in a variety of locations below the Mason-Dixon Line. Some of this wealth was later retrieved, but most of it, perhaps several million dollars' worth of gold and silver coins, remains hidden.

One such cache, or more accurately, series of caches, represented an astoundingly rich source of gold that had been held during a portion of the war in a temporary treasury headquarters in Richmond, Virginia. When it became clear that the days of the Confederacy were numbered, military leaders decided to hide the gold so it would not fall into the hands of Union forces. Captain J. W. Duchase, commander of Company C of the Fourth Mississippi Infantry stationed in Richmond, was charged with removing the South's store of gold coins to another state and hiding it in predetermined locations.

Duchase was roused from his sleep at two o'clock one crisp autumn morning in 1864 and told to report to headquarters. There, he found officers and aides frantically preparing to abandon the area in the wake of news that the Yankees were closing in and time was growing short.

Duchase, along with his entire company, was ordered to report to the railway station at 6:30 that evening. Each man was told to pack three days' worth of rations, at least forty rounds of ammunition, and full marching gear.

That evening, Captain Duchase and the seventy-eight fighting men from Mississippi who made up his infantry company assembled at the station platform. The train idling on the tracks consisted of a locomotive, four boxcars, and three flatcars. The boxcars contained arms, ammunition, and other material the Confederate leaders thought prudent to ship out. The end flatcar held a three-inch bore field piece, some other armament, and a detachment of gunners. The two remaining flatcars were loaded with iron cooking pots, each filled with gold coins, each lid tightly fastened with wire.

As Duchase waited with his men next to the train, he was delivered a set of orders and told to open them only when he arrived at his assigned destination—Greensboro, North Carolina. Duchase's personal notes on the incident explain what occurred next:

We traveled all night and reached Greensboro the next day at 4 p.m. There I opened my orders and found the following instructions: "You are to proceed the following night to McLeansville by way of the North Carolina Railroad. After leaving McLeansville, you will bury these pots in groups of three on each side of the R.R. and not over one hundred paces from the right of way. In case there are houses nearby, proceed further. Also, plot the burial places as nearly as possible."

Duchase and his men followed the orders to the letter, burying the pots in lots of three. In all, they covered sixteen miles along the railroad tracks between Greensboro and Company Shops (later renamed Burlington). During the caching of the gold-filled pots, Duchase made specific notes on the location of each burial.

Their mission complete, Duchase and his infantry company rode the train into Company Shops, turned it around, and returned to Greensboro. From Greensboro, they traveled by another train toward Richmond to submit the information on the locations of the buried Confederate gold and to aid in the defense of that city against Yankee attack. Along the way, however, the train was derailed by a Union blockade and most of Company C was captured. Duchase and one lieutenant escaped, but in the process they lost the precise description of the burial locations of the Rebel gold.

Duchase and the lieutenant lived in hiding for several weeks and were forced to steal and beg food from isolated farms they encountered in the area. Union troops eventually found the two men. Near starvation, they were huddling behind a fallen log hoping to go unnoticed when they were recaptured. They were interrogated and then sent to a Yankee prison camp where they waited out the remainder of the war.

When the South surrendered, Duchase, along with thousands of other captured Rebels, was freed. As soon as he could manage, he traveled to Mexico, where he became involved in mining and real estate. Over the years he prospered from a number of successful ventures, married a Mexican woman, and raised a family. Duchase often thought of returning to North Carolina and retrieving the Confederate gold he'd buried. The former infantry captain believed he remembered enough of the area between Greensboro and McLeansville to locate the treasure easily. Business concerns and family matters, however, occupied his time, and he was unable to travel. While living in Mexico, Duchase wrote extensive notes in a journal about the war in general and his assignment to hide the Confederate gold in particular. His descriptions of where he hid the gold-filled iron cooking pots were clear and precise.

More time passed. Duchase's wealth grew, and his desire to return to North Carolina waned. One day during the 1890s, Duchase met a man named P. H. Black who was traveling through Mexico. When Duchase learned Black was from Greensboro, North Carolina, he told him his story. Black was fascinated by the tale and wanted to learn more. In response, Duchase gathered up his notes on the war, along with an account of the buried gold, and turned them over to his new friend.

Duchase passed away in Mexico around the turn of the century. He never left the country after arriving there in 1865. P. H. Black died in North Carolina during the 1930s. It remains unknown what became of the notes Duchase passed along to him. Nor does anyone know whether or not Black attempted to retrieve any of the gold. If he did, he never commented on it. If, by chance, he found some of the caches, he certainly did not locate them all.

During the 1880s, Burlington grew to become an important settlement in that part of the Appalachian Piedmont. In the fields and meadows along the old North Carolina Railroad tracks, farmers worked to meet the growing demand for cotton and corn. Late one summer afternoon in 1910, a black farmhand was plowing in a field about three miles west of Burlington. The mule-drawn plowing was tedious, and the day was warm. Both man and horse were tired and looking forward to quitting time when the steel plow struck something hard, breaking its point. The farmhand, grateful for the opportunity to stop plowing for a few minutes, dug into the ground and retrieved a rusted iron cooking pot wrapped tightly with thick wire. He wrestled the heavy pot out of the ground and onto the surface. After untying the wire and removing the lid, he was surprised to find the vessel filled to the top with twenty-dollar gold pieces. The farmhand made the discovery approximately one hundred paces from the railroad tracks.

Not knowing the true value of the coins, the farmhand took several of them into Burlington the next day and traded them for dimes. The twenty-dollar gold pieces aroused local curiosity, and the laborer was questioned about his discovery. Before sundown of that same day, the cornfield where he found the gold coins was swarming with men digging into the rich soil, searching for more. Within two feet of where the first iron pot was found, the landowner found two more. Though he never revealed to anyone the value of his discovery, from that day on he was a wealthy man.

The three pots of gold that were found in the cornfield by the farmhand and his employees came about as a result of a lucky accident. Others may have been found in the same manner, but they have never been recorded. It is a certainty that hundreds of the iron cooking pots, each filled to the top with gold coins, are still buried near the railroad tracks.

During the mid-1990s, an amateur treasure hunter who lived in Tennessee contacted me, identified himself, and explained that he had designed what he referred to as a revolutionary new type of metal detector. He was vitally interested in the pots of Confederate gold buried near the old NCRR tracks and was convinced he would be able to find some of them with his new invention. He asked if I could offer any additional information regarding the locations of the gold-filled pots. I shared what I had. Three months later the man called me back and reported that he had located and retrieved six of the pots. The two separate finds were each one hundred paces from the old tracks, each in an abandoned field. A few weeks later, he mailed me a sizeable check that he explained was a "consultation fee" for helping him with his discovery. Over the next three years, the same man found six more pots. In 2001, I learned that the treasure hunter had passed away, leaving his family an impressive inheritance.

In 2010, I was contacted by two different groups of treasure hunters, each with the goal of continuing the search for more of the pots of gold. At this writing I am still waiting to hear the results of their expeditions.

CHAPTER TWENTY-ONE

The Lost Gold of Cohutta Mountain

TO THE SURPRISE OF MANY, THERE IS A LOT OF GOLD TO BE FOUND IN the Georgia Appalachians. Most people associate gold mining with the western United States, but prior to the great American Gold Rush of the 1850s, most of the gold mined in the United States came from the Appalachian Mountains, which spread across North Carolina, South Carolina, and Georgia. Eons ago, when this great mountain range was taking shape, tectonic forces deep beneath the crust were activated. Molten rock under tremendous pressure surged upward and fought to break through the crust and spread out across the landscape. For the most part, the crust held, keeping the magma trapped beneath thousands of feet of rock, where it began to cool. This suppressed volcanic material eventually hardened to form granite and related rock. Scattered here and there within the vast underground bodies of this igneous intrusive stone, impressive veins of gold-filled quartz were formed.

With the passage of millennia, pressures within the earth forced some of the granite masses closer to the surface. Ages of erosion by wind and water removed hundreds of feet of sedimentary overburden, eventually exposing the ancient granite and its pockets of gold.

As streams flowed across the exposed granite, eroding the coarse surface particle by particle, more of the entrapped minerals were exposed. Early Indians who settled in this region often found gold in these mountains, sometimes in great quantity. They mined it, occasionally stored significant quantities of it, and used it primarily for making ornaments and jewelry.

When white trappers and traders arrived in the Georgia Appalachians, they saw the fine gold jewelry worn by the natives. They craved to know where it came from and how they could obtain some of it.

Soon prospectors and miners arrived. While exploring throughout the mountain range, they relocated many of the mines used by the Indians and discovered several other outcrops of gold-laden quartz. Mining enterprises were established, and soon the range was teeming with others hopeful of making their fortunes. When most of the Indians were removed from the region during the 1830s, more greedy and enterprising whites encroached onto the lands formerly occupied by the Indians and began extracting the riches from the rock in great quantities. Several tales of impressive gold deposits have come from the area near Cohutta Mountain, two and a half miles east of Chatsworth, Georgia, near the Tennessee border.

Prior to the Indian removal of the 1830s, a man named William Hassler constructed a grist mill on the creek that still bears his name. Hassler had settled in the shadow of Cohutta Mountain several years earlier and made friends with all the Indians living nearby.

The largest of the Indian villages was spread out over the flood plain of Hassler Creek just east of the mill. Hassler ground corn for the Indians and also traded items he had shipped from Virginia. When he first began dealing with the Indians, he noted that they seemed to have a lot of gold, and he requested payment in that metal.

Hassler noted that whenever the Indians ran low on gold, three or four of the elders would leave the village and travel along the creek upstream toward Cohutta Mountain. They were usually gone for less than a week, and when they returned they carried leather ore sacks filled with gold nuggets that were quite pure.

It was clear to Hassler that the Indians had a productive gold mine somewhere in the mountains, and he was determined to learn its location. One day when he spotted four tribal elders departing the village for Cohutta Mountain, he called for one of his slaves. The miller told the young man to follow the Indians at a discreet distance and try to locate their gold mine.

For most of the day the slave followed the elders, staying well behind and just out of sight. When he reached the base of Cohutta Mountain, he lost sight of the Indians and could not relocate their trail. As he searched the ground for some sign of passage, the four elders appeared out of the surrounding forest and encircled him. They warned him that if he ever followed them again he, along with his entire family, would be killed. The Indians marched the young slave back to the mill and presented him to Hassler with the same warning. With that, the elders turned and trotted back up the creek toward the mountain. Several days later, Hassler saw them returning with more sacks full of gold nuggets. The Indians carried on their trade with the miller as though nothing had happened. With the threat of death hanging over him, Hassler never again attempted to find the Indians' gold mine.

Years later, during a lull in the War between the States, two soldiers named Pence and Wells were granted a short leave to return to their homes near Cohutta Mountain for a seasonal hog roundup. As their story has been reconstructed, the two men were walking alongside a narrow stream on the mountain when they chanced on the old Indian gold mine. Each man dug several ounces of ore out of the gold-laced quartz they found inside the mine and, with full pockets, set out in search of more stray hogs.

Once all the livestock was rounded up, Pence and Wells, by agreement, had to return to their military unit. They put the gold in a shot pouch and hid it in the hollow of a chestnut tree on the mountain. They planned to return to the mine to harvest more of the gold after they served their required time in the Confederate army. When they returned to their unit, they told several of their fellow soldiers about discovering the gold mine.

During the ensuing months, Wells was killed in action and Pence was wounded badly enough to merit a discharge. The trauma of the war apparently affected Pence's mind to the degree that he had difficulty sleeping and remembering things. His neighbors claimed he had simply gone crazy as a result of his experiences.

Several months after returning to his Georgia home, Pence made a marginal recovery. He recalled the time he and his friend Wells found the gold mine and decided to take the long walk from his home into the mountains to retrieve the pouch of gold nuggets hidden in the tree. He planned to exchange the ore for money, purchase some mining equipment, and extract more gold from the old Indian mine. Pence searched for several days but could never locate the correct tree. He told others that the tree was no longer there, but it is more likely that he simply could not find it.

For the rest of his life, Pence tried to relocate the ancient gold mine. According to relatives, years of fruitless searching caused him to completely lose his mind. To the last, Pence never wavered in his belief in his tale of finding the mine with his friend Wells. Now and then, one of the ex-Confederate soldiers who had been told the story of the mine by Pence and Wells would arrive at Cohutta Mountain to search for it. None were successful.

During the first decade of the 1900s, an elderly Cherokee Indian showed up in the town of Chatsworth. The old man was little more than a derelict, clothed in tattered rags, barefoot, and hungry. He tried to secure work at several places but was chased away. On his second day in town, he struck up a conversation with a group of men and told them that if they would give him $600, he would lead them to the secret Indian gold mine on Cohutta Mountain. Two of the men—James Mullins and Jim Sellers—knew the story of the mine, were aware of Pence's attempts to relocate it, and decided to take the risk.

The following morning, the Indian led Mullins and Sellers to Cohutta Mountain on horseback. For a day and a half, they traveled up ravines and narrow valleys into regions the two white men had never seen, though they had been to the mountain many times on hunting trips. As they rode, Mullins and Sellers carefully noted landmarks so that they could return to the mine, should it be found, without the help of the Indian.

Midway through the second day, the three men rode right up to the gold mine. Dismounting and tying their horses to nearby trees, the two white men entered the low, narrow shaft and dug out enough gold to fill their saddlebags. The Indian remained behind to tend to the horses.

When their packs were filled, Mullins and Sellers followed the Indian out of the mountain and back to Chatsworth. Pleased with the deal they made, they paid off the Indian, who immediately left town and was never seen again.

Mullins and Sellers were now rich men as a result of exchanging the gold for currency. Inexperienced with possessing wealth, the two spent lavishly on horses and good times. Nine months later, their money was gone, and they began planning a return trip to Cohutta Mountain and the old Indian gold mine.

On the morning of the second day out of Chatsworth, Mullins and Sellers got lost. They recognized none of the landmarks nor the trails and became hopelessly confused. After spending another full day trying to get their bearings, they gave up and returned to Chatsworth without having relocated the mine. They made several more attempts to find it but were never successful.

During the 1930s, a man named Fletcher arrived in the vicinity of Cohutta Mountain and spent a lot of time prospecting around its flanks. Fletcher was originally from England and had come to the United States for the express purpose of seeking his fortune in the gold fields of Georgia. By the time he arrived, many of the productive mines had closed down, and he heard a lot of talk about how the ore had been mined out. Undaunted, Fletcher decided to try his luck on and around Cohutta Mountain.

After several trips to the mountain, Fletcher returned to Chatsworth with an impressive sack of gold nuggets. He claimed he dug the gold out of an old abandoned mine he found near a creek on the mountain.

Several weeks later, Fletcher fell ill and was given only days to live. Just before he died, he requested that his bed be taken outside where he could look at the mountain. He gave what gold he had left to a newfound friend who had ministered to him during his time of illness. Fletcher explained to his friend that inside the mine was a wide vein of quartz woven with one-eighth-inch-thick strands of the purest gold he had ever seen. Fletcher gave his friend directions to the mine. The friend, however, did not write them down, and after the passage of a few days he could not remember them.

One week later, Fletcher died. With his passing went the knowledge of the secret location of the old gold mine. Though many have attempted to relocate it over the past several decades, none have been successful.

CHAPTER TWENTY-TWO

Civil War Outlaw Treasure Cave

FOR GENERATIONS, CAVES HAVE BEEN FAVORED BY OUTLAWS AS HIDE-outs. There was nothing to construct—a gang could just move into the cave and set up temporary residence. Caves offered simple yet effective protection against the elements. They were cooler in the summer and relatively warm in the winter. They were normally found far from settled areas, thus providing isolation away from the prying eyes of area residents. In addition, caves were often ideal places to hide stolen loot and goods.

One such cave exists in Henderson County in western North Carolina. A study of the area history shows that this location often served as a temporary home for outlaws and as a repository for stolen gold, silver, and currency. History has not, however, revealed whether any of the hidden treasure has been recovered from this cave. To this day, it is believed that a fabulous treasure lies within this former outlaw hideout. The problem is no one knows exactly where it is.

Knowledge of the Henderson County treasure cave came to light with the discovery of the diary of Lieutenant J. H. Hadley, a Union army officer. Hadley's company fought with Confederate forces during the famous Battle of the Wilderness in 1864 in eastern Virginia. During the early stages of the fighting, Hadley was wounded and captured and, along with hundreds of other Union prisoners, shipped by rail to Columbia, South Carolina, where he was interred in a prison camp.

The camp was a makeshift assemblage of poorly constructed shacks in a disease-ridden swamp. Each day, men died from dysentery and malaria. Not wanting to end their lives in this dreadful confinement,

Hadley and three companions decided to take their chances and began to hatch a plot to escape.

One night, the four men managed to break out of the prison and flee into the nearby woods. Days later and out of range of pursuit, they undertook a long journey northward in hopes of encountering a Union encampment along the way. For two weeks, the men made their way through woods and across open meadows, trying to remain hidden and always on the alert for Confederate patrols.

From time to time they set snares for rabbits and managed to subsist on small game and wild fruits. More often than not, however, they went hungry. Their boots soon wore out and had to be discarded. Eventually, the difficult travel and the constant hunger began to take a toll, slowing the fugitives' journey. An unusually cold autumn overtook them as they crossed the border into North Carolina.

With the frigid temperatures, wild fruits grew scarce and game less plentiful. The men resorted to raiding the vegetable cellars of farmsteads they encountered. Where possible, they would also steal chickens. During one raid on a garden patch containing some greens and root crops that had not been killed by the frost, the four men were surprised by three women who arrived to harvest the vegetables. The women were armed, and they leveled their rifles at the intruders. While the escapees were held at gunpoint, the youngest woman ran back up the trail in search of help.

Several minutes later, a tall, bearded old man returned with the woman. He was carrying a rifle and appeared irritated at finding the men in his garden. He noted the ragged and torn Union army uniforms on the haggard-looking, barefooted men and told them he had no use for Yankees or thieves. He moved as though he intended to shoot the four of them on the spot. Hadley and his companions dropped to their knees and begged for their lives. They told the man they intended no harm and only needed a little food for themselves and would leave immediately.

Pondering the situation for a moment, the old man lowered his rifle. His demeanor changed from rage to pity for the Yankees. Though he was a born and bred Southerner who was committed to the Confederate cause, even losing two sons to the war, it was difficult for him to watch anyone suffer. The thought of turning away hungry men repulsed him.

Relenting, he invited the fugitives to his cabin, where he saw to it that they were fed a proper meal.

During the dinner, the old man suggested to Hadley that it might be prudent to hire a guide to lead them to the closest Union encampment. He said he knew a man who might deliver them to Knoxville for one hundred dollars in gold coins. Hadley agreed to the proposition, the man was sent for, and he arrived at the cabin late the next day. According to Hadley's notes, the newcomer was a quiet, thin, dark man who wore a black bowler hat that shaded much of his face. After listening to the fugitives' tales of escape and flight through the wilderness, he agreed to let Hadley pay the one hundred dollars in gold on arrival at Knoxville since none of the escapees possessed any money. He told the four he would return with horses just after sundown the following evening.

The sun had been down for an hour when a quiet knock was heard on the cabin door. This was followed by a voice that announced all was ready and that they must leave at once. When Hadley and his companions assembled outside the cabin, the guide informed them that they would be blindfolded and that they would soon understand the reason for the precaution. After they were blindfolded, each man was helped onto a horse, and they were led into the woods. As they rode along, Hadley made mental notes of the journey. He later recalled that they crossed two shallow creeks near the end of the ride. Eventually, the guide called a halt and the four blindfolded men were helped off the horses. Following a brief hike up a moderately steep gravel slope, they were led to a guide rope. At the end of the rope the men came to realize they were inside a large cave. After several more minutes of walking, they were ordered to halt and their blindfolds were removed.

Looking around, Hadley saw that they were in a dark cavern lit by three torches placed in cracks in the walls. He could hear water dripping a short distance away. Occasionally, he heard voices coming from some distant part of the cave. As his eyes adjusted to the dim light, he saw several saddlebags and wooden chests piled against the far wall of the chamber.

The guide handed each man a blanket and suggested they get some sleep because they would depart early in the morning. He explained that the four of them would have this chamber to themselves, but they were not to leave it. He said a guard was stationed in the passageway with orders to shoot anyone who tried to leave the cave.

During the night, Hadley found it difficult to sleep. He threw aside his blanket, removed one of the burning torches from a niche in the cave wall, and explored the chamber. When he arrived at the pile of saddlebags and chests at the far wall, he scanned them with interest. Hadley noted the chests were the type used by railroad companies to transport gold, silver, and currency. Bending to one of the saddlebags, he unfastened the straps, pulled back the flap, and peered into it. His heart pounded at what he saw: inside were hundreds of gold coins. He opened several more of the packs and found gold or silver coins in each. He assumed that the chests also held gold and silver. Hadley began to understand the need for the blindfolds—he and his companions were being held in a cave used by bandits to store treasure. Hadley refastened the saddlebags and returned to his blanket but could not sleep.

Early the next morning, six rough-looking men entered the chamber. Hadley realized they were the men he had heard from somewhere deep in the cave the night before. Each was carrying a heavy saddlebag that was added to the pile at the far wall. Pretending to be asleep, Hadley listened to the conversations of the newcomers. Thus, he learned that they were robbers and smugglers and that the cave was used as a repository for their booty.

A few minutes later, the guide entered the chamber and told the four fugitives that it was time to leave. He explained that the six men who had arrived minutes earlier would accompany them to Knoxville, deliver them to a Yankee camp, and collect the one hundred dollars in gold.

Again, Hadley and his companions were blindfolded and led from the cave. Once outside, they were ordered to stop and rest at a grove of trees where the horses were tied. As they waited, they could hear the sounds of labored breathing from the outlaws and the movement of heavy rocks. As he waited, Hadley managed to adjust his blindfold such that he could see what the men were doing. The bandits were sealing the entrance to the cave by piling boulders in front of the opening, closing it off and making it look much like the rest of the talus-covered slope.

When this was done, the outlaws gathered in front of the cave and swore an oath of secrecy about the location of the treasure.

Minutes later, all were mounted and riding north. After traveling a few miles, the guide told the escapees they could remove their blindfolds. After doing so, Hadley glanced about in an attempt to locate some prominent landmarks, but all he was able to see was a dense growth of beech trees where they stopped for a few minutes to rest the horses. After continuing, they rode into a thick oak forest. The remainder of the trip was uneventful, and a few days later the party reached the outskirts of Knoxville and a Union army camp.

The bandits held one of the fugitives hostage and told Hadley and the two others to go into the camp, obtain the promised one hundred dollars, and return as soon as possible. On reaching the camp, Hadley and his two friends were escorted to the tent of a company commander, where they related the story of their capture, imprisonment, escape, flight across the countryside, and subsequent recapture by the bandits. Following some initial disbelief and cross-interrogation by the commander, Hadley's tale was accepted and the order given to a corporal to procure one hundred dollars in gold coins. As it turned out, there was no gold in the camp, and the corporal returned with one hundred dollars in paper currency. The commander sent Hadley off in the company of two armed soldiers to make the exchange.

The bandits were understandably nervous when Hadley returned in the company of an armed escort. When they were offered the paper money instead of the gold they demanded, they grew furious. Hadley explained there was no gold in camp and pleaded for the outlaws to accept the money and release his friends. The discussion grew heated, and one of the bandits pulled a pistol and fired at one of the troopers, killing him instantly. While Hadley and the hostage took cover, the rest of the outlaws pulled their weapons and shot at the second trooper, who took shelter behind a tree. Frustrated, the outlaws wheeled their horses around and raced back toward the south.

Hearing the gunshots, the company commander assembled two dozen troops and set out in pursuit of the outlaws. About five miles from the hostage exchange site, the soldiers overtook the fleeing bandits and a gunfight ensued. Following half an hour of exchanging rifle fire, all the outlaws lay dead. When the outcome was reported to Hadley later that day, he realized that all the men who knew the secret location of the treasure cave were dead.

When the war ended two years later, Hadley returned to Henderson County to search for the cave. With some difficulty, he located the small farm where he and his companions were first discovered. He looked up the old farmer who had fed them and arranged their escape. He thanked him again for saving their lives.

Hadley was certain the treasure cave was still sealed and the gold and silver coins lay untouched within the large chamber where he had first seen them. He was given permission to set up a small camp near the cabin, and he spent the next several weeks walking and riding throughout the countryside in search of the cave. With no substantive visual landmarks to guide him, Hadley had difficulty retracing the route he had followed blindfolded and on horseback two years earlier. Following a series of failures, Hadley gave up and returned to his home.

Hadley came back to Henderson County to search for the cave and its treasure several times over the next twenty years, but each trip was no more successful than the first. He never found the elusive treasure cave. Years later, on his deathbed, Hadley said he was certain the cave had never been reopened and the treasure was still intact.

Using Hadley's notes, others have attempted to follow the cryptic and convoluted directions, but to date none of the treasure has ever been recovered. Most estimates place the value of the treasure at several million dollars.

CHAPTER TWENTY-THREE

John Crismo's Lost Treasure

EARLY ONE MORNING IN 1887 ON A REMOTE RANCH NEAR PECOS, TEXAS, a young cowhand was trying to wake his bunkhouse companion, an elderly employee named John Crismo. When Crismo did not respond to the call, the boy walked over to his bunk and tried to shake him awake. The old man was dead.

The ranch foreman was summoned and a burial arranged. A few days later, as the owner of the ranch searched through Crismo's meager belongings for the name of a relative, he chanced upon a well-worn diary. The little book held fascinating details of a buried treasure, one that today may be worth $4 million yet still lies buried beneath a few inches of soil and rock on a lonely mountainside in western Virginia. The ranch owner pored through the often-unintelligible handwriting in Crismo's diary and over several weeks pieced together the story of the buried fortune.

In 1846, when the United States declared war on Mexico, a very young John Crismo enlisted in the army in his home state of New York. Before leaving for foreign soil, Crismo became engaged to a local girl, and they agreed to marry when his enlistment was over. While Crismo was in Mexico, however, his betrothed fell ill, dying only a few days before he returned.

Crismo never recovered from the loss of his sweetheart. He visited her grave, then mounted his horse and rode out of New York, never to return. For years, the young man roamed the wilderness of Pennsylvania and Ohio, keeping to himself and living like an Indian deep in the woods. He craved neither the sight nor the company of others.

When the Civil War erupted, Crismo, wishing to return to combat, rode eastward into Pennsylvania and enlisted in the Union army. He was assigned to a cavalry regiment that was immediately ordered to Virginia.

Crismo's unit engaged in several raids on farms and small communities in western Virginia, capturing livestock and confiscating food, arms, and ammunition and often filling their pockets with stolen money. In time, the cavalry force grew to become little more than a gang of bandits robbing and looting its way across the Appalachian landscape.

One day, the unit was ordered to patrol an area in southwestern Virginia in Tazewell County. The command, twenty-four in number, camped on the side of a mountain that overlooked a long, narrow valley. The valley floor was flat with rich soil and highly productive. At one end of it was a mansion, and the prospect of finding something of value in the fine home appealed to the troopers.

The valley and everything in it belonged to an eccentric wealthy man named James Grierson. Grierson, who had inherited one fortune, made another from cotton and livestock. The old bachelor owned thirty slaves and was thought to be the wealthiest man in western Virginia. He was reputed to be worth over $1 million, a staggering amount at the time.

When the Civil War broke out, Grierson, concerned about the safety of his fortune, withdrew all his money from the area banks and converted it into gold coins. With the help of his favorite slave, Grierson packed the coins into canvas bags and buried them behind his barn.

Anticipating an easy and successful raid, Crismo and the other cavalrymen rode into the valley and up to Grierson's farm. They took the owner prisoner and hung him by the wrists from a tree limb in his front yard. Throughout an intense and sometimes brutal interrogation, Grierson steadfastly refused to reveal where he had buried his fortune. It soon became clear to the Union riders that the old man preferred death to parting with his gold. Grierson did not survive the interrogation.

During the time Grierson was being questioned, Crismo befriended the old slave who had helped Grierson bury his fortune. With some cajoling and the promise of freedom, Crismo convinced the slave to show him where the gold was buried. The slave took Crismo behind the barn, dug two feet into the ground, and pulled up one of the heavy sacks of coins. After examining it, Crismo told the slave not to tell any of the other cavalrymen about the treasure.

Several days later, Crismo's unit was assigned to another area several miles way. Once they had arrived and established camp and were awaiting further orders, Crismo rode back to the Grierson farm under cover of night. He found the old slave, and together the two men dug up the sack of coins buried behind the barn. The two men loaded the gold-filled sacks onto a pair of stout workhorses and transported them back to the camp on the side of the mountain where the unit was located before riding on to the Grierson plantation. A short distance from the campground, Crismo and the slave dug a deep, wide hole, deposited the coins into it, and refilled it, covering the cache with rocks and forest debris. Following this, they started out for the current campground. On the way, Crismo handed the slave a handful of gold coins and gave the man his freedom.

On returning to his unit, Crismo told none of his fellow troopers about the Grierson fortune. That night, by the dim light of the campfire, Crismo sketched a crude map showing the location of the treasure cache in his diary. In his rough and clumsy grammar, he added descriptions of the terrain and pertinent landmarks. The next day, the cavalry unit left Tazewell County for a new assignment in the eastern part of the state.

As the war raged on, Crismo's unit fought in several skirmishes. In one, Crismo was seriously wounded. Following a lengthy recovery in a field hospital, he was granted an honorable discharge and sent on his way. His first thought was to return to Tazewell County and dig up the gold, but continuing military action there would have made it difficult. Crismo packed up his few belongings and traveled westward, roaming the country and gradually regaining his health while biding his time until he could return to Virginia and retrieve the buried treasure.

For many years, Crismo wandered the sparsely settled regions west of the Mississippi River, eventually finding his way to Texas. Traveling from town to town and taking odd jobs, the former Union cavalryman barely earned enough to survive. His few diary entries during this time suggest that the wound Crismo had suffered was giving him some serious problems and causing great pain. His writing also suggested that he was not mentally sound.

Years passed, and Crismo eventually landed a job as a cowhand on a ranch near Pecos, Texas. Though much older than most of the other cowboys and quite infirm, he proved a consistent and loyal worker up to the day he quietly passed away in his sleep.

———

During the years that followed Crismo's death, his diary passed through several hands and eventually wound up in the possession of a Pecos County man who decided to go in search of the cache of buried gold coins. Using the clumsily drawn, faded, and somewhat vague map, the searcher arrived at a small Virginia settlement called Aberdeen. Just north of this hamlet, the man located the long, narrow valley that had once been part of the extensive Grierson estate. The land was now state property, having reverted to government ownership when Grierson passed away leaving no heirs.

Just north of the old Grierson plantation was a prominent mountain, undoubtedly the one on which Crismo and his cavalry unit camped before riding onto the farm. After exploring around the mountain for several days, the searcher discovered what he was convinced must have been an old military campsite. He found two Union army–issue canteens, numerous shell casings, and other items suggesting a temporary cavalry bivouac. While Crismo's directions were clear enough to this point, his diary entries never actually said on which side of the camp he buried the gold coins. For weeks, the treasure hunter searched the area. Experiencing one disappointment after another, he finally gave up and went back to West Texas. Crismo's diary was relegated to a high, dusty shelf in a storeroom and in time was lost. The searcher never again attempted to locate the treasure.

Others have searched for John Crismo's buried gold coins. A number of so-called experts, employing metal detectors and dowsing rods, have combed the mountainside near the old cavalry camp attempting to find what is estimated to be a $4 million cache of gold coins. The treasure remains hidden to this day.

CHAPTER TWENTY-FOUR

Poor Valley Treasure

DURING THE YEARS PRIOR TO THE CIVIL WAR, ABRAHAM SMITH AND his two sons, Eli and Samuel, owned and operated one of the largest and most successful plantations in western Virginia. Not far from the Smith farm and near the Clinch Mountains was a place called Poor Valley. Here could be found a large saltworks in which the Smith family had an interest. The vast works was the source of much of the salt for that part of the South and was also a primary supplier for the army of the Confederacy. Nearby was a small community called Saltville in which lived some of the salt mine workers. Smith, distrustful of banks like most Southerners, insisted on payment in gold and silver coins for his salt and plantation products. These coins, along with the family jewelry, were kept in a small chest in one of the many closets in his home.

Early on the morning of October 2, 1864, Abraham Smith received word that a large contingent of Union cavalry led by the ruthless General George Stoneman was approaching the valley. Smith was aware of the soldiers' penchant for raiding and looting homes and farms, stealing family savings and treasures. He decided to hide his fortune lest the enemy seize it. Smith hurriedly loaded his chest of coins onto a wagon, drove out toward the salt mines in Poor Valley, and buried it in the middle of the road near the tiny community of Saltville.

Unknown to Smith, Stoneman had orders to destroy the saltworks, thus disrupting the Rebel army supply and creating economic havoc in the area. He led his Union force into the valley late that morning only moments after Smith buried his wealth.

General George Stoneman
PEE WEE KOLB

Based on scouting reports, Stoneman anticipated little resistance in the valley. He was therefore surprised when a large combined force of area residents and Confederate soldiers met him. Earlier, Southern scouts had warned citizens of the approaching Yankees. The hastily assembled force of farmers, farm laborers, salt workers, and Confederate soldiers engaged the Union cavalry in a fierce battle. After nearly one hour of fighting, Stoneman called for a retreat. The inexperienced but enthusiastic Southerners pursued the famous cavalry leader and his troop back through Cumberland Pass and into Kentucky.

After the skirmish, Eli Smith could not be found. He was not among the dead and wounded, and it was assumed he was captured by the Yankees and executed along the trail during the disorganized retreat. A search party was assembled to look for the body, but after several days of combing the woods on both sides of the road and having no success, it was disbanded.

Several days after the battle, Abraham Smith and his son Samuel returned to the roadbed only to find that the chest filled with coins and jewels had been dug up and removed, presumably by Yankee soldiers. The shock of losing a son and his entire fortune within the space of a few days was too much for the elderly Smith. His health, along with his will to live, deteriorated rapidly. A year and a half later, Abraham Smith passed away a broken man.

Years later, Samuel Smith received a strange letter. It was addressed to his late father but was dated nearly two years earlier. It was from a Corporal Allen E. Brooks, formerly of Stoneman's cavalry unit that invaded Poor Valley. The message surprised and shocked Samuel—it explained what happened to his brother Eli and the cache of family treasure. It read:

Kind Sir:

I am in pain and upon my deathbed, but I feel I must divest my conscience of a burden that has kept constant company with my soul since shortly after we fought over the saltworks there. Your son, Eli, fearing he would be hanged, made a deal with my first sergeant, Jack Harrington, to share your fortune with him, an amount of some $46,000 in gold and silver coins, $12,000 in jewelry, and several gold watches. In return your son was to be helped to escape into Tennessee. Your son was not killed during the fighting, Harrington murdered him later on the pretext that he was escaping. With my help, Harrington removed the cache and hid it in a saltpeter cave, about a quarter of a mile distant from the little town church. Harrington was accidentally killed in a blast while we were destroying the saltpeter caves before we abandoned the area. I took a Minnie ball at the Battle of Seven Mile Ford and have been unable to travel since. I had planned to return to Saltville and reveal the location of your money to you. But I am dying and I want you to know that I took no part in the murder of your son.

Respectfully,
Corporal Allen E. Brooks
Late of the Fortieth Mounted Infantry
Army of the U.S.
General Stoneman Commanding

Using the letter from Corporal Brooks as a guide, Samuel Smith tried several times to find the treasure. The saltpeter caves were located in Poor Valley between Allison's Gap and Saltville. Many caves in the area had been blasted shut and otherwise destroyed by Stoneman's troops during the battle at the saltworks. Removing the debris from the entrances of all of them turned out to be a formidable task for Samuel Smith. His efforts to find the treasure proved to be in vain, and he eventually gave up and moved away.

Several who have researched this tale over the years were convinced that the Smith treasure was still hidden in one of the saltpeter caves called Harmon's Cave. The closed entrance was breached and the cave entered, but all attempts at finding the total of $58,000 worth of gold and silver coins and jewels (in 1862 values) have failed. There are several other caves nearby, and it is probable that the lost treasure still reposes on the floor of some deep chamber in one of them.

CHAPTER TWENTY-FIVE

The Lost Treasure of the Gray Ghost

COLONEL JOHN SINGLETON MOSBY WAS ONE OF THE MORE FAMOUS, AND likely one of the most colorful, leaders of the Confederate army during the Civil War. Mosby was a graduate of the University of Virginia and a practicing lawyer. He enlisted in the Southern army as a private at the outbreak of the war. After serving as a scout for General J. E. B. Stuart during the Peninsula Campaign and earning recognition for valor at the battles of Bull Run and Antietam, Mosby quickly rose in rank to colonel. In 1863, he organized and led a guerilla unit called Mosby's Raiders. With his team of fearless fighting men, he conducted a campaign of harassment and predation against Union forces in Maryland and Virginia. So effective were the raiders that Mosby's name became legendary. Union soldiers, who had no success whatsoever in pursuing or capturing the guerillas, began referring to Mosby as the Gray Ghost, an appellation by which he is still known.

During the spring of 1863, Mosby captured $350,000 worth of gold, silver, jewelry, and other valuable items during a desperate flight from Yankee pursuit. He buried the booty in a secret location in Virginia's Farquier County in the Appalachian Piedmont. There it rests today, tempting treasure hunters who come from near and far to try to find it.

Mosby and his raiders had attacked the Fairfax County, Virginia, courthouse not far from Washington, D.C., where they surprised and captured Union general Edwin H. Stoughton. Though a general, Stoughton was never regarded as much of a leader by other Union officers or by historians. Stoughton has been described as overweight and overbearing, and he possessed a great appetite for fine foods, wine, and women. He lacked the enthusiasm for combat and avoided it as much as possible. When Colonel Mosby and his handpicked guerillas entered the courthouse, they found Stoughton surrounded by casks of wine and great stores of food. Weeks earlier, Stoughton had taken over the courthouse and was using it as his private quarters for the duration of the war. In spite of the bloody conflict swirling around him, the hedonistic general saw to it that he wanted for little during those trying times, preferring to send his officers and troops out into the field to perform the work of the military.

Though Stoughton was guarded by two captains and thirty-eight enlisted men, the experienced raiders took him with ease. At the same time, Mosby captured fifty-eight horses, several carriages, numerous crates of victuals and drink, and $350,000 worth of gold and silver, coins, jewelry, plates, and tableware that Stoughton's soldiers had looted from Southern homes. Colonel Mosby had all the valuables gathered up and placed in several canvas bags.

Learning that several Union forces were in the area searching for him, Mosby ordered his guerillas to load the booty into the carriages. With Stoughton and his men as prisoners, they fled southwest toward the town of Culpepper, where General Stuart awaited them.

Mosby's Raiders, along with captives and cargo, raced through the rolling hills of the Appalachian Piedmont, a low, eroded plateau that offered a transition from the rugged highlands to the gentle lay of the coastal plain.

When the guerilla force crossed into Farquier County, one of Mosby's advance scouts raced back to the colonel with the news that a Union cavalry contingent was bearing down on them from the northeast. Because the captured goods were slowing the retreat to Culpepper, Mosby decided to ditch the barrels of wine and crates of food. He also elected to bury the canvas sacks filled with treasure.

By Mosby's later recollection, the raiders halted briefly about midway between the towns of Haymarket and New Baltimore to unload the excess baggage. While his soldiers quickly dumped the cargo from the carriages, Mosby, accompanied by his trusted sergeant James F. Ames,

General John Singleton Mosby
PEE WEE KOLB

carried the sacks of gold, silver, and other valuables some distance from the trail and placed them in a hastily dug, shallow hole between two tall pine trees. After filling the hole, Mosby notched several tree trunks with his knife so the site could be easily identified on a return visit.

Mosby expected to come back to this area within a few days and retrieve the treasure, but the war kept him busy and carried him farther and farther from Farquier County. When the war was over, Mosby returned to his law practice and settled in western Virginia far from where he fought during the conflict. He never returned to the Piedmont to retrieve the treasure.

Mosby, as well as some members of his guerilla unit, often related the story of burying the treasure along the rocky trail during the flight from the Fairfax courthouse. Though many were aware of this cached fortune, only Mosby and Ames knew the exact location. Sergeant Ames, however, would never have an opportunity to reveal the secret. During the war, he was captured by General George Armstrong Custer and hanged at Fort Royal.

When asked why he never returned for the treasure, John S. Mosby, the famed Gray Ghost and Confederate War hero, would always evade the question and change the subject. When he was eighty-three years old and near death, the question of the buried treasure was raised again.

The Gray Ghost responded: "I've always meant to return to the area and look for that cache we buried after capturing Stoughton. Some of the most precious heirlooms of old Virginia were buried there. I guess that one of these days someone will find it."

Today, the cached canvas sacks filled with gold, silver, jewelry, and other valuable items hidden by Mosby and Ames on that spring day in 1863 would be worth several million dollars. Employing old maps, journals, and military records, a number of treasure hunters have attempted to retrace Mosby's retreat from the Fairfax courthouse to the rendezvous with General Stuart at Culpepper, but none could ever be certain of the route.

Over the years, tales of hikers and hunters encountering two very old pine trees with markings and blazes in that same area have been related. When informed of the potential connection between the marked trees and a fabulous treasure cache, those who had encountered the trees were never able to relocate them. There is little doubt among researchers that the Gray Ghost's treasure still lies there today under only a few inches of soil.

Chapter Twenty-Six

Buckhannon River Valley Treasure

DURING THE HEIGHT OF THE CIVIL WAR, A SOLDIER WHOSE NAME HAS been lost to history stopped by the Wilson farm in a sparsely settled region of West Virginia's Monongahela County. The soldier and farmer Wilson were friends, and he and his wife invited the soldier to spend the night.

Curious as to why his friend was not with his military unit, Wilson asked several pointed questions. The soldier explained that he was on temporary leave and then related an amazing tale of a hidden treasure for which he was searching. The immense fortune was reputed to be buried in a lost cave in the upper reaches of the Buckhannon River Valley, about fifty miles from their present location and to the south in Upshur County.

The soldier had just returned from Upshur County, where he had been thwarted in his search by roving bands of outlaws and military patrols, all of which made travel through the remote and unprotected West Virginia wilderness difficult if not impossible.

Following the evening meal, when Wilson and the soldier were alone, the guest opened his leather traveling bag and withdrew an eighteen-square-inch parchment map. He showed the map to Wilson and pointed to a location where he said he believed the treasure was hidden. The soldier told his host a story about a party of miners that had been transporting silver ingots eastward when they were set upon by a band of Indians. While fleeing, the miners found refuge in a cave and buried the ingots in the far corner of a large chamber. In the dark of night, the miners silently crept from their hiding place and continued their journey. They intended to return someday and retrieve their fortune. According to the soldier, the miners never returned, and the treasure still lay in the cave. The map they were examining had been made by one of the miners. He was drowned in a rain-swollen river during an attempt to return to the cave. The map, explained the soldier, was useless without the key, which was held by a close friend who lived just to the west in Marion County. Exactly what the key consisted of was never made clear. It is presumed that it was a detailed explanation of elements of the map.

Wilson got caught up in the soldier's enthusiasm for finding the hidden treasure, and before the night was over the two men agreed to become partners. They made plans to obtain the key and then set out in search of the treasure together. The soldier, however, was overdue in reporting back to his cavalry unit and said he needed to be on his way. Leaving the map with Wilson, the soldier gave directions to the Marion County resident with the map key. He asked Wilson not to wait for him to return but to go ahead and pursue the search on his own if he did not come back in a reasonable time after the war ended. With a few parting words, the soldier rode away into the woods. Wilson never saw him again.

Wilson waited for nearly two years after the end of the war for the return of his partner. Finally realizing that it was unlikely he would ever show up, he decided to travel to Marion County and obtain the key. He packed a wagon, hitched up two stout horses, and at the last minute invited his grandson, Joseph, along. The trip through the rugged and often dangerous wilderness was long and hard and turned out to be an unforgettable experience for the younger Wilson.

Decades later, when Joseph A. Wilson was himself a grandfather, he related to relatives a story about the arduous trip he undertook through the Appalachian backcountry in search of a lost treasure. It rained often, and the swollen streams made crossings difficult and dangerous. The wagon and team occasionally bogged down in the mud, and the two men had to slog through muck and high water to help pull the horses free. The younger Wilson recalled that at one point during the return trip, his grandfather told him he now had the key necessary to find the lost treasure. He explained that they would return home and rest themselves and the horses for a few days, then repack for another expedition to find

Lucullus Virgil McWhorter
PEE WEE KOLB

the cave. On arriving back at the farm, however, the elder Wilson became sick and died within a few days.

Because of his youth and inexperience, Joseph Wilson had little inkling of the real or potential worth of the buried treasure that his grandfather talked about. He understood nothing of the map and the key that could supposedly lead him to the cave. Several years later, when he developed an appreciation for the value of money, he recalled his grandfather's quest. He also recalled that his grandfather was a very conservative man and not one to waste time. The fact that he had traveled across two counties to obtain a key to the treasure map suggested to the young Wilson that the old man thought it very important.

Joseph Wilson's family moved to another valley, but when he was old enough, he went to his grandmother's home and asked her about the map and key left by his late grandfather. A map should be obvious enough, but he had no notion of what form the key took. He presumed it consisted of a paper or papers containing crucial information. After searching through several drawers, old trunks, and bundles of papers, he found the map. Carefully unrolling it, Wilson noted that it was of a very old and stiff parchment. The inscriptions on the map were finely written in ink, and while clear and easy to read, they were vague about the amount and type of treasure. Nothing on the map explained the origin of the treasure or who buried it.

Diligent searching failed to turn up the key. The grandmother, who could neither read nor write, confessed that she might have burned it years earlier along with some other papers she deemed unimportant.

After several weeks of studying the map, Wilson determined that the treasure had long ago been hidden in a cave not far from the old Seneca War Trail where it crossed the upper part of the Buckhannon River in Upshur County. According to the map, the trail could be seen from the cave's low entrance.

Without the key, Joseph Wilson searched for the treasure cave several times but never found it. After years of effort, he gave up. In 1891, he turned the map over to a man named Lucullus Virgil McWhorter, a native of the town of Buckhannon. McWhorter was one of the few formally educated men living in the area at the time. During the early 1880s, McWhorter had conducted a detailed study of local Indian artifacts and campgrounds. Wilson gave McWhorter the map because the latter seemed keenly interested in local history. Wilson also told McWhorter what he knew of the origin of the map and of the lost key. McWhorter was fascinated with the tale of lost treasure and attempted to find it himself several times but with no success. In 1915, McWhorter published an account of the lost treasure cave.

Many others, using the old parchment map or copies of it, have searched for the lost treasure cave over the years, but none have ever found it. Researchers have diligently pursued an explanation for the origin of the treasure but have come to no definitive conclusion. Some, however, have reason to believe it might have been part of a shipment of silver ingots from one of the legendary Jonathan Swift mines that were worked during the mid-1700s.

Members of the Swift party often passed through the Buckhannon River Valley on their way to and from the famous but elusive mines in Kentucky. Jonathan Swift himself makes several references to the area in his journals. One particular entry by Swift may shed some light on the lost treasure.

While establishing a camp along what many believe was the Buckhannon River, the Swift party was attacked by Indians. Quickly strapping the packs of ingots and equipment onto their mules, the miners fled along the Seneca Trail, eventually taking refuge in a cave near the headwaters of the river. While several men guarded the entrance, others buried the bars of silver. Relieved of their heavy load, the miners waited until darkness and then escaped, intending someday to return and retrieve the wealth secreted in some dark chamber of the cave. As far as anyone knows, they never did.

It is also worth noting that Swift, in his journals, occasionally referred to the rich silver mines in the Buckhannon River Valley that he and his men worked in 1761. It is possible that the silver in question may have been taken from one of those mines before being cached in the lost cave.

Throughout the upper part of the Buckhannon River Valley, many old mining tools have been found, and some suspect that they may have belonged to the Swift party. In addition, at least two very old mine shafts have been found. The entrances had been covered over in an attempt at concealment. Years of erosion, however, have exposed the openings.

These days, few people have reason to travel to the relatively isolated reaches of the upper Buckhannon River Valley in Upshur County. The local tales and legends of lost mines and buried treasures are relatively unknown to outsiders. As a result, there have been few organized attempts to find the lost cave. Continued research and systematic exploration of the area might someday yield one of the country's richest treasure caches.

CHAPTER TWENTY-SEVEN

Abandoned Union Payroll

FAYETTE COUNTY, WEST VIRGINIA, WAS THE SETTING FOR A GREAT deal of military traffic during the Civil War as both Union and Confederate soldiers passed through the area. At one point, a contingent of Yankee soldiers was escorting a large payroll—a wagon loaded with gold coins packed into several canvas bags—to a Federal encampment nearby. Details are sketchy, but it is known that as the party traveled along the winding mountain trails through the dense woods, scouts informed the commanding officers that a Confederate patrol was approaching at a rapid speed from the east.

The Union officer ordered the escort into a full gallop in the hope of outdistancing the Rebels, but after attempting to elude the enemy for almost five miles, it became clear that they would be overtaken. Anticipating a skirmish, the officer halted the wagon and ordered the canvas bags that held the Union payroll taken from the vehicle and buried a short distance from the trail. While troopers hastily excavated a shallow pit into which the gold was placed, the officer made notes of the surrounding environment and landmarks in his personal journal. He wrote that the payroll was cached in a location on the west side of the Buyandotte River not far from the small settlement of Chapmanville.

Once the hole was refilled and covered with forest debris to make the location look much like the rest of the area, the soldiers remounted and rode on. One hour later, they were overtaken by the Confederate patrol, which opened fire on spotting their enemy. The Yankees sought cover behind rocks and trees and fought back, but they were disorganized, ill prepared, and outnumbered. The fighting lasted for two hours, and when it was over, all the Yankees lay dead.

The Rebel soldiers searched the wagon for the money they knew it was carrying and found it empty. Suspecting the gold coins had been buried somewhere along the trail shortly before the engagement, they retraced the Yankees' route for several miles. They found nothing.

Returning to the site of the skirmish, the Confederates stripped the Union soldiers of anything of value, including weapons, ammunition, boots, and clothes. An unknown soldier found the officer's journal and, without reading it, placed it in his knapsack. He carried the journal with him during the remainder of his enlistment. Months later, on returning to his home in Tennessee, he placed it in a trunk. During all that time, the soldier never read the journal.

During the early 1930s, a descendant of the Rebel soldier found the old journal in the trunk, read it, and decided to undertake a search for the buried Union payroll. Though the search lasted for several days, nothing was found.

The directions in the old journal stated that the payroll coins were buried at a point where the old road and the Buyandotte River came within twenty yards of one another. Since the war, however, the road has been all but obliterated by a modern thoroughfare. In addition, the river has shifted its course several yards in this area.

Today, the Union payroll would represent an immense fortune in gold coins. Assuming it was not uncovered by the shifting river and washed downstream, this important Civil War cache is probably still lying where it was buried, only a few inches below the surface not far from Chapmanville, West Virginia.

CHAPTER TWENTY-EIGHT

Confederate Treasure in North Carolina

ONE OF NORTH CAROLINA'S MORE INTERESTING CIVIL WAR ENCOUN-ters was called the Battle for Fort Macon. Prior to this 1862 fight, Union troops assembled on a portion of the mainland coast where the present-day town of Morehead City is now located. From this point, the low horizon of Bogue Bank, a narrow barrier island separating Bogue Sound from the Atlantic Ocean, could be seen just south of the sound.

Fort Macon, the target for the scheduled Union assault, was located on the eastern end of the small island. Not far from where the Union soldiers stood near the shoreline, a treasure estimated to be worth tens of thousands of dollars was buried prior to their crossing the sound. Years later, only one man was left alive who remembered where the treasure was buried. He died while attempting to return to it. The location remains lost to this day.

Fort Macon, which overlooks a portion of North Carolina's coast, was originally constructed by the Federals. Fewer than twenty soldiers generally occupied it at any given time. Both Yankees and Rebels regarded the small fort as having strategic importance. Because of reduced Union manpower, the Confederates gained control of the fort in 1861 when Captain Josiah Pender, accompanied by a force of fifty troops, captured it. For more than a year, Pender's army remained in command of Fort Macon and kept their canons pointed toward the open waters of the Atlantic Ocean, ready to defend against an attack from a Union armada.

In April 1862, Union general Ambrose Burnside received orders to retake Fort Macon from the Confederates as soon as possible. At the time, Burnside expressed some concern with the assignment because none of the young soldiers in his company of two hundred men had ever seen battle. The general was bothered by the notion that this significant lack of experience could jeopardize the operation. Burnside, a shrewd military strategist, decided to learn all he could about the fort and its occupants. He sent his trusted scouts to the area to study the position of the bastion and the geography of the land. Meanwhile, Burnside subjected his young troopers to intensive training in preparation for the coming assault.

Several days later, Burnside learned from his scouts that Fort Macon was situated on the eastern end of a barrier island called Bogue Banks and that it was separated from the mainland by approximately one mile of open water. The scouts also noted that all the fort's canons were pointed toward the ocean in anticipation of an assault from that direction. After thoroughly considering the situation, Burnside decided to launch a surprise attack on the fort from the rear. On the following morning, the general put several men to work constructing rafts stout enough to float canons and troopers across the canal.

Early on the morning of the planned attack, Burnside's troops massed at the point of land where Morehead City now rests. While the general discussed last-minute battle preparations with his lieutenants, Sergeant Gore, a thirty-five-year-old veteran of several skirmishes, addressed the assembled soldiers. Walking among the rows and columns of troops, Gore instructed each of them to remove rings, watches, jewelry, and money and place the items in a sack that was to be buried in a secret location just prior to departing for battle. The general, Gore informed the soldiers, did not want any valuables to fall into the hands of the Confederates. The truth, however, was that Burnside had no knowledge whatsoever of Gore's plan.

When some of the troopers resisted turning over their valuables to the sergeant, Gore suggested they appoint one man they could trust to accompany him to the secret location. The soldiers quickly elected Joseph Poindexter, a young private from Pennsylvania. Moments after collecting

General Ambrose Burnside
PEE WEE KOLB

the items, Gore and Poindexter disappeared into the nearby woods. Once out of sight of the other soldiers, they buried the heavy sack among the roots of a large cedar tree. It is estimated that several thousand dollars' worth of money and jewelry were cached.

A short time later, the rafts carrying men and canons were launched into the sound and rowed toward Fort Macon. Two hours later, when they landed on the beach a short distance north of the fort, the soldiers hastened to set up the canons. Soon afterward, a furious bombardment of the Confederate bastion was underway. When it appeared as though the Rebel defenders were significantly weakened, Burnside ordered his soldiers over the walls to charge the fort. Moments earlier, he had given them instructions to kill or capture the Confederates.

During the ensuing fight inside the fort, dozens of both Union and Confederate soldiers were killed. Eventually, however, the Rebels were forced to retreat, and the fort once again fell into the hands of the Union forces.

While counting the dead, Union soldiers noted that Private Poindexter had been shot in the back of the head. Many were convinced that Sergeant Gore had murdered the young trooper during the assault on the fort. They suspected Gore planned to return alone to the buried treasure cache with the intention of removing the valuables for himself. Though there was much grumbling among the troopers, not a single one was willing to level a formal accusation at the sergeant.

As the soldiers debated among themselves about how best to deal with the situation, Burnside suddenly received orders to return to the mainland and lend support to a Union company engaged in a fierce battle with Rebel forces several miles away. Following a hasty assembly, the troops, accompanied by Burnside, rowed back across the sound and headed inland. Sergeant Gore was given a command of ten soldiers and placed in charge of Fort Macon. The following day, however, most of the soldiers accompanying General Burnside were killed during the fighting.

Sergeant Gore remained at Fort Macon for the duration of the Civil War. During the last few months of the conflict, the sergeant became very ill and often lapsed into fits of coughing. When the South finally surrendered in 1865, Gore decided the time was appropriate to return to the mainland and dig up the treasure he had cached three years earlier.

Weakened by his sickness, Gore asked a local fisherman to row him to the North Carolina shore. Gore and the fisherman had become friends during the preceding months and spent a great deal of time together drinking and playing cards. On the way to the mainland, Gore, in between fits of coughing, told the fisherman about the buried treasure and offered to split it with him.

As Gore was rowed across the sound by his friend, he described the site where he buried the treasure years earlier. He spoke of a large cedar tree not far from the shoreline with numerous thick, exposed roots. The treasure, he claimed, was buried only a few inches deep. Gore also confessed to this friend the circumstances leading up to caching the treasure and of his deception.

When the rowboat skidded onto the beach, Gore attempted to climb out but was seized by a sudden fit of coughing. After several minutes, he collapsed backward into the skiff. Concerned that the ex-soldier could die before leading him to the location of the buried treasure, the fisherman carried Gore to the home of a nearby doctor. After examining the sergeant, the doctor diagnosed him with typhoid fever. Gore never regained consciousness and died the following morning.

Several years later, the fisherman returned to the area where Gore claimed the treasure was buried. To his dismay, he encountered hundreds of large cedar trees with exposed roots and nothing in particular to distinguish one from the other. After digging around the bases of several of them and finding nothing, he gave up and eventually forgot about the treasure.

As far as is known, the bag of valuables buried by Sergeant Gore has never been recovered. The growth and expansion of Morehead City has undoubtedly accounted for a great deal of change in the surrounding environment. In spite of that, many continue to maintain that not far from the shoreline located east of the city is buried a small fortune in rings, watches, and other items from the Civil War.

CHAPTER TWENTY-NINE

Sunken Civil War Firearms

CLOSE TO MIDNIGHT ON OCTOBER 21, 1862, THE COMMERCIAL SHIP *Minho* chugged slowly along the southern margin of Sullivans Island, a small barrier islet located near the entrance to South Carolina's Charleston Harbor. For five months, the *Minho* had successively penetrated blockades set up by Union ships and delivered its precious cargo to Southern customers.

The *Minho* did not carry ordinary cargo. Stored in the hull of the vessel were two hundred tons of rich transport, including cases of imported wines, fine silks, expensive glass and china, and valuable medicines, all of which had been hard to obtain since the beginning of the war. Wealthy Southerners who were determined not to alter their lavish lifestyles as a result of the raging conflict paid high prices for these items transported by the *Minho*. Unknown to many at the time, the *Minho* also carried a shipment of firearms destined for the Confederate army. Dozens of crates of Enfield rifles were stored in the hull in containers disguised as toolboxes. In addition, there were several smaller crates of ammunition.

The iron-hulled *Minho* was constructed in Scotland eight years earlier. At 175 feet long with a four-hundred-ton displacement and a state-of-the-art steam propeller engine, the ship was fast and maneuverable, features deemed invaluable while running the Union blockades. The *Minho* was purchased by Frasier, Trenholm, and Company, a shipping enterprise that owned a number of vessels that carried goods from Europe to the United States and back.

George Wigg, a representative of the shipping company, learned that wealthy landowners in the South were willing to pay premium prices for certain valuable and hard-to-obtain imported goods. Sensing a high-profit market, Wigg arranged to have a variety of such goods transported to Bermuda, loaded onto the *Minho*, and carried to selected American ports along the Atlantic coasts. There, it was clandestinely sold to the customers. The only obstacle, realized Wigg, was the seizure by Federal vessels that had been ordered to stop all shipments to Southern ports. Wigg, however, convinced the shipping company owners that the potential profit was well worth the risk.

The *Minho's* captain had previously delivered goods to the port of Charleston and was very familiar with the harbor. After arriving from an easterly direction, he planned to navigate the vessel along the southern margin of Sullivans Island until arriving at the harbor's entrance. At that point, he had a good view of most of the anchorage. If Union warships were spotted, the captain would merely steer the *Minho* out to sea, fire the boilers, and outrun the slower ships. If, on the other hand, the harbor was clear of any blockade, he would dock the ship, quickly unload the goods, and be away in a matter of a few hours.

As the *Minho* rounded the western tip of Sullivans Island, the captain, along with the lookouts, examined the boat traffic around Charleston, approximately three and a half miles away. At first they did not detect the small fleet of Federal warships lying less than a mile to their starboard and near the northern tip of the island.

Moments later, a lookout spotted the Union gunboats and sounded a warning. As the captain turned the vessel toward the Atlantic, however, three more Federal ships were spotted approaching from the south, effectively cutting off escape. Realizing there was no chance in a fight, and fearing for the fate of the crew as captives of the Federal army, the captain of the *Minho* pointed the vessel toward Bowman's Jetty, a six-hundred-foot-long ridge of partially submerged rocks extending into Charleston Harbor from Sullivans Island. Moments later, amid the noise of shattering hull plates, the *Minho* slammed into the rocks and skidded onto the top of the ridge. The ship's officers and crew quickly abandoned the vessel, leaping into the surrounding water and swimming to the nearby shore.

Completely unmanned and with gaping holes in its hull, the *Minho* took on water and settled onto the jetty rocks.

Because of the war and the growing presence of Union troops and ships in the area, no immediate attempt was made to recover any of the cargo that had been aboard the *Minho*. When Frasier, Trenholm, and Company learned that the original consignment was virtually intact, they requested and received permission to attempt a salvage recovery.

After spending several weeks trying to refloat the *Minho*, the owners finally determined it would not be possible. Days after abandoning the project, they sold the vessel, along with its entire contents, for only $6,000. The new owners, a group of Charleston businessmen, recovered approximately 75 percent of the cargo, including the wine, china, and medicines. During the following weeks, all the goods were auctioned off to Charleston residents. During the salvage process, none of the rifles were recovered.

For just over ten years, the wrecked *Minho* remained lodged on the rocks of the jetty. Inside the broken, water-filled hull, some of the original cargo remained untouched. Several crates of Enfield rifles were among the unrecovered goods. In 1873, the U.S. Army Corps of Engineers, while in the process of modifying Bowman's Jetty, pulled the *Minho*'s remains from its position and allowed it to settle onto the bottom of the harbor.

During the early 1980s, South Carolina's Institute of Archeology and Anthropology became interested in the historical significance of three sunken ships near Bowman's Jetty, one of them being the *Minho*. In December 1985, the institute issued a salvage license that permitted recovery of lost cargo from the remains of the vessels. During the process, divers working around the hulk of the *Minho* discovered a case of twenty rifles. After the long-submerged firearms were hauled to the surface, they were identified as Enfields. Based on some concentrated research, it was eventually learned that the case was part of a secret shipment carried by the vessel and intended for Confederate troops.

Several days later, a second crate of Enfields was recovered near the wreck. Scattered about the bottom sands of the harbor next to the crate, salvors retrieved more than one thousand bullets.

Salvage activity was postponed during the 1987–1988 winter storm season. When it was resumed in April 1988, divers were delighted to discover that storm-generated currents had surged through the *Minho*'s interior and cleaned it of a heavy deposit of sand. During the first dive, two more crates of rifles were discovered along with hundreds of bullets. Over the next few days, three more full cases of Enfields were located. Because of equipment difficulties, however, not all the crates were raised to the surface.

Salvage and recovery operations were stalled in 1989 when Hurricane Hugo struck the region. As a result of the storm, millions of tons of sand were shifted around on the bottom of the harbor, and a great deal of it covered the *Minho*. During subsequent dives to the wreck, more crates of rifles were located, but none could be recovered. Since that time, the ever-shifting sands, along with the termination of salvage licenses, have inhibited further recovery activities.

No one knows for certain how many crates of Enfield rifles were originally aboard the *Minho* when it slammed into Bowman's Jetty. As a result, no one knows how many still remain at the bottom of the harbor. Experts estimate that it may be as many as one hundred. Rifles such as these, Civil War artifacts a century and a half old and in good condition, would bring extremely high prices from collectors. Offers for some of the recovered Enfield rifles have exceeded $1,500 apiece in the past. Should this value remain constant or grow, the rifles remaining at the bottom of the Charleston Harbor, if recovered, could bring in well over $1 million.

CHAPTER THIRTY

Confederate Silver Cache in Pennsylvania

DURING 1864, THE CONFEDERATE ARMY WAS EXPERIENCING INCREAS-ing difficulty maintaining sufficient funds in the treasury for the purchase of arms, ammunition, and supplies. In addition, the lack of money was presenting another significant problem, and that was meeting the payroll for the soldiers in the field. Though documentation is sketchy, there exists enough information to support the notion that a train carrying tons of silver ingots intended to supplement the Rebel treasury was traveling through western New York State when it was stopped and robbed. The silver, estimated to be worth several million dollars at the time, never arrived in the South. Some have argued that if the South had received this shipment of silver, and had been able to provide more and better arms and ammunition, the outcome of the war might have been different.

Nevertheless, the whereabouts of this great treasure remained a mystery for twenty years. After that time it was found and then lost again.

As the train approached a remote location in western New York, eighteen men, all mounted on sturdy horses, were hiding in a grove of trees. Their attention was focused on the treasure the train was transporting—millions of dollars' worth of silver ingots. The light of a full moon glinted off the railroad tracks. The apprehensive horsemen eyed a large boulder that had been moved onto the rails. The rock was positioned such that the engineer could see it in time to stop. If he did not, the train would derail.

At the last moment, the engineer spotted the boulder and applied the brakes. But it was too late. Though the speed of the train was dramatically reduced, it was still going much too fast to prevent the impending disaster. The engine slammed into the rock with such force that it, along with the two following cars, was knocked off the track. At that moment, the eighteen horsemen pulled bandannas over their faces, broke from cover, and spurred their mounts toward the disabled train. They carried rifles and pistols.

Dazed and injured railroad employees were rounded up and placed under guard. Four of the riders rode straight to a certain boxcar, broke open the wooden door, and climbed inside. There they found the target of their robbery: inside the boxcar were hundreds, perhaps thousands, of silver ingots. Once stacked neatly against one wall of the boxcar, they were now strewn about the floor as a result of the violent collision.

One of the men picked up an ingot and noted it was stamped with an inscription: "Government Genuine. New York City." A moment later, the leader of the gang flashed a signal toward the nearby woods. Seconds later, a caravan consisting of a dozen stout wagons, each pulled by a team of horses, filed out of their hiding place and headed toward the boxcar.

It required most of the night to transfer all the silver ingots from the train into the wagons. When the job was completed, the wagon drivers drove the vehicles across the railroad tracks and onto a little-used dirt road that led into Pennsylvania a few miles away. By the time the sun rose above the treetops, the wagons bearing the silver bars were fifteen miles from the scene of the crime. It was two full days before investigators arrived at the site of the wreck, but by then the trail was cold.

The amount of silver taken from the boxcar that night has been estimated to be at least 20 tons, with some researchers insisting the amount was closer to 115 tons.

For years, aspects of the western New York train robbery incident remained shrouded in mystery. The source of the silver was never discovered, although some researchers are convinced that it was gathered and contributed by Northern businessmen who were sympathetic to the Confederate cause. After being loaded onto the train, it was to be clandestinely shipped to some unidentified location in the South. Others have advanced the notion that the silver was stolen from a Federal depository. No report of such a theft, however, has been found.

The eighteen men who robbed the train have never been identified, but it seems that they were in possession of accurate intelligence and that they operated in a disciplined, almost military, manner. The location to which the fortune in silver ingots was transported and for what purpose also remains a mystery, but two years after the robbery, evidence surfaced that suggested it was hidden in a remote cave in Fayette County in southwestern Pennsylvania.

Fayette County lies upon a geologic substrate of thinly bedded and highly jointed limestone, conditions that are conducive to the formation of caverns. Indeed, it has been estimated that hundreds of natural caves exist in this region. Laurel Caverns, a popular tourist and recreation destination, lies only five miles southeast from downtown Uniontown in Forbes State Forest.

During the mid-1800s, an elderly, white-haired, reclusive trapper named Dobbs lived in a crude cabin of his own making near Laurel Caverns. Dobbs generally avoided contact with others and was rarely seen by his few neighbors. He survived principally by foraging for nuts and berries in the woods, snaring rabbits, and trading the few pelts he acquired with his rusty traps for staples such as salt, coffee, and sugar in Uniontown. About once every month, Dobbs would walk into town and trade for a small sack full of tinned goods. Now and then, he agreed to work odd jobs here or on nearby farms. The money he was paid was usually used to purchase liquor.

One day in 1866, Dobbs arrived in town, went to the mercantile, which also served as a grocery store, and filled up an old canvas bag with meats, cheeses, and tins of tomatoes and fish. Surprised, the grocer, who had known Dobbs for years, asked how he planned to pay for it all. In return, Dobbs handed the proprietor a silver ingot. Astonished at the large, heavy bar, the grocer inquired of the trapper how he had happened onto such riches. Dobbs casually replied that he had found a cave filled with hundreds of the ingots. The grocer noted that the ingot was stamped with "Government Genuine. New York City."

Bennett H. Young
PEE WEE KOLB

Once every month thereafter, Dobbs arrived in Uniontown to purchase food and other supplies. He always paid with a silver ingot. It was recorded that each of the bars was stamped with the same inscription. Dobbs's quality of life had improved significantly.

A few Uniontown residents noticed Dobbs's sudden wealth, and at times the old man was followed after he made his purchases and headed back into the woods. When he suspected someone was on his trail, Dobbs would leave the road and make his way through the thick forest, often doubling back on his tracks to confuse any who might be intent on finding where his ingots were stored. Dobbs never approached the cave where the ingots were hidden when he thought someone might be observing him.

In 1869, a group of four hunters rode into Uniontown and made purchases at the mercantile and the local taverns, paying with bars of silver that bore the same inscription as those of Dobbs. When asked, the hunters claimed they found the bars, along with thousands of others, in a remote cave a few miles southeast of town. They said they intended to return for the rest and live the remainder of their lives as wealthy men.

The following morning, the hunters rode out of Uniontown and were never seen again. It was never known if they returned to the cave and retrieved more of the silver bars. In 1871, four skeletons were found in the woods not far from Laurel Caverns, and many are convinced that Dobbs discovered the hunters taking silver from the cave and killed them.

A few weeks after the skeletons were found, Dobbs arrived in Uniontown and announced to all that no one would ever be able to find his fortune because he had moved it to a different location. It was discovered later that Dobbs had moved out of his cabin. His new residence was unknown.

One day in 1872, Dobbs came into town to make his usual purchases. That evening, he went to a local tavern where he had too much to drink and told an acquaintance that he had transferred all the silver bars from the cave where he found them to a new location—an abandoned coal mine. So remote was this mine, said Dobbs, that no one would ever be able to find it.

Dobbs continued to come into Uniontown once a month to buy supplies, a pattern that he followed for the next two years. Then, one month he didn't show up. Nor did he the next month, nor the next. In fact, Dobbs was never seen in Uniontown again, and the residents assumed that the old man had met with a fatal accident or finally succumbed to old age. For months afterward, several Uniontown citizens would undertake a search to try to find the abandoned coal mine where Dobbs claimed he had cached his treasure, but none were successful.

During the summer of 1873, a man many believed to be Dobbs showed up at Latrobe, a small town some thirty-five miles northeast of Uniontown. The old man, with long white hair and a generally unkempt appearance, lived under porches and in alleys. He solicited handouts from Latrobe residents, who regarded him as a vagrant but generally treated him kindly.

When the old man would finally acquire enough money to purchase a few drinks, he could be seen in the local tavern where, inebriated, he would relate a strange story of how he came to lose a fortune in silver ingots.

According to a story attributed to the stranger, he had been living above an abandoned coal mine. Deep within it, he said, he had hidden hundreds of bars of silver. The mine collapsed, burying the bars under uncountable tons of rock. Though the old man tried for weeks to dig through the rubble and reach his cache, he eventually realized it was hopeless.

For another year, the old man lived in Latrobe on handouts and odd jobs. One morning he was found dead in an alley and given a pauper's burial. It was never learned for certain if the unfortunate fellow was the reclusive Dobbs who once lived near Uniontown and who was wealthy beyond imagination. The man in Latrobe died penniless.

Considering the evidence, there is no basis on which to reject Dobbs's claim that he found a large cache of silver ingots. During the 1970s, a California-based treasure-hunting company arrived in southwestern Pennsylvania to conduct research on the tale. Finally convinced that an impressive fortune in silver bars lay in a collapsed coal mine somewhere in the region, they undertook a deliberate and organized search. Several such mines were located, some dating back to the mid-nineteenth century. Several bores were sunk into these mines in the hope of locating some evidence of the silver, but none was found.

There is no reason to believe that any of Dobbs's lost silver ingots have been found. It is likewise easy to conclude that they still lie deep within the collapsed coal mine of which the old man spoke. It is also logical to assume that the collapsed coal mine was located not too far from the original hiding place near Laurel Cavern, for the task of transferring what amounted to several tons of silver ingots would have been immense for only one man.

The minimum estimate of the amount of silver buried in the collapsed coal mine is twenty tons, give or take the thirty or so bars that Dobbs and the four hunters used to pay for purchases in Uniontown. If twenty tons of silver are buried there (and there may be more, much more) the value of this lost cache has been estimated to be no less than $3 million and perhaps as much as $18 million to $20 million.

Dobbs's collapsed coal mine would have originally been a shaft dug with hand tools, since the heavy equipment used for strip mining did not exist at that time. If the old mine could ever be identified with certainty, it may be possible to bring large earth-moving equipment to the site to uncover it. This would require a significant investment in time and money, but the rewards would be impressive.

Chapter Thirty-One

Lost Confederate Treasure Cache in Vermont

AMERICA'S CIVIL WAR, 1861–1865, WAS FOUGHT OVER THE QUESTION of states' rights and a number of significant differences in ideologies as they related to economics and slavery. In all, eleven states seceded from the Union and organized into the Confederate States of America. As such, they attempted to create a separate country, a plan that was doomed from the start.

The sites of battles and skirmishes between the North and the South, important victories and crushing defeats, have been made into national and state parks. The locations of lesser skirmishes between these two forces have been identified and preserved and in many cases made available for tourism, historical research, and recreation.

Many are aware of major battle sites throughout parts of the North and South, but few associate Civil War–related skirmishes with the northeastern state of Vermont and the country of Canada. In 1864, however, a partial company of Confederate soldiers raided a small New England town, stole a fortune in gold from its banks, and fled north into Canada. Most of the gold, all in coin, was buried somewhere along the escape route near the Canadian border. It has never been found, and the search for it continues to this day.

Just past midnight on October 18, 1864, a contingent of twenty-five Confederate soldiers broke camp along the banks of Lake Champlain's Missiquoi Bay, saddled their horses, mounted up, and rode single file southward down a narrow road leading from the Canadian province of Quebec into Vermont. The morning was cold, the dew heavy on the grass and brush, the riders silent. The only sound that could be heard was the jingling of metal harness fittings and the occasional blow of a horse.

The abbreviated company was led by Captain Bennett H. Young. The destination was St. Albans; a small, quiet village located less than twenty miles from the international border in northwestern Vermont.

Though the Confederacy was composed primarily of Southern states, the governors of this resistance maintained a presence in eastern Canada. From this vantage point, safe from the intrusion of the Northern army, Southerners courted the Canadians as well as friendly Europeans, soliciting monies for arms and ammunition in order to carry out the struggle. By 1864, however, things were looking grim for the South, and desperation raids by small Rebel armies were common. But none had ever occurred this far north of the Mason-Dixon Line.

Young's Confederate command was one of several stationed in Canada. On October 15, the captain received coded intelligence describing how large deposits of gold coins totaling $200,000 had been made in each of the three banks in St. Albans. With the South badly in need of money to plug deep holes in the Confederate treasury, Young and his troops were ordered to loot the Yankee banks and move the gold to Canada. From there, it was to be shipped to Richmond, Virginia, the home of the Confederate treasury.

Just as the morning sun illumined the tree line east of St. Albans, the Young-led troopers galloped into town, firing weapons and screaming Rebel yells. With little trouble, they forced their way into the banks, located the $200,000 in gold coins, and crammed it into saddlebags. As they strapped the heavy leather bags onto spare horses appropriated from a nearby corral, the citizens of St. Albans, awakened by the commotion, were loading their weapons and preparing to defend the village against the mysterious raiders. Before the St. Albans residents could determine what was happening, the Rebels, still shooting off their weapons, set fire to the three banks, mounted up, and escaped northward. The entire raid took less than thirty minutes.

By the time the Confederate soldiers were picking up speed on their way out of town, armed St. Albanites were pouring into the streets searching for something to shoot at. Several shots were fired at the retreating horsemen, but none found their mark. Return fire from the soldiers, however, hit two residents. One was killed, the other seriously wounded.

Along the trail north of town, Young, fearful of pursuit, urged his soldiers to greater speed. He was desperate to get his command back across the border before an effective posse could be organized. Within minutes after the robbery, however, about thirty angry and vengeance-minded St. Albans citizens were already whipping their horses along the same trail taken by the fleeing bank robbers.

Up ahead of the pursuers, the raiders were experiencing serious problems with the pack animals they were using. The horses, unaccustomed to carrying the heavy weight, were tiring and slowing down. Further, the Confederates were unskilled at close-herding the animals, and the frenzied activity made the horses skittish. Every now and then one of the horses would break away only to be chased down and returned to the column. On at least two occasions, the command was forced to stop when some of the hastily secured gold-filled saddlebags broke loose and fell to the ground.

The troops had reached a point about two miles from the border when Young shouted a command to halt. Concerned about the recurring problems slowing down the escape and acutely aware that the pursuers were only minutes away, Young ordered several of the saddlebags removed from the horses and buried in a pine grove he spotted just off the trail. With haste, five troopers excavated a shallow hole, placed the saddlebags within, and covered them over.

Nearby was a large, flat rock. Young enlisted four of the men to carry the huge rock to the cache and place it over the top. The soldiers struggled with the burden but finally succeeded in dropping the rock on top of the site. At that moment, Young heard the sound of pursuit on the trail behind them. Quickly, the Rebels mounted up and quirted their horses northward.

A short time later, the Confederates crossed the Canadian border with the posse in sight behind them. Believing they were safe, the Rebel troops slowed their animals to a walk, turned, and jeered at the Vermonters they believed they had just outwitted. Much to Young's surprise, however, the St. Albanites did not stop at the border. They did not even pause. Instead, they quirted their horses to greater speeds in an attempt to reach the bank robbers. With the angry Vermonters almost on top of them, Young's soldiers, now in fear for their lives, tried to coax their own mounts to greater speeds.

Within seconds, three of the Southerners fell to Yankee bullets. Young, believing his only chance for survival was to turn and fight, ordered his men to draw their weapons and make a stand. During the ensuing skirmish, ten more Rebels were killed and eleven captured. Only three managed to escape.

When the saddlebags were searched, the Vermonters found only $80,000 of the stolen gold coins. They deduced that the Confederates must have buried the rest somewhere along the route. On the return trip, the posse members scanned both sides of the trail for some sign of a recent excavation or a likely place to cache several saddlebags' worth of gold but found nothing. None of the captured Rebel soldiers were members of the detail that was assigned to bury the gold, so they were unable to provide any insight into the location. The search for the missing coins continued for weeks but was finally abandoned when it appeared hopeless.

The details of the Confederate raid on St. Albans were widely reported. As time passed, the tale was relegated to a minor role in the history of the Green Mountain State and, save for those who lost money or suffered the deaths of relatives, was soon forgotten.

In 1868, a former Confederate soldier lay dying from tuberculosis in a Greenville, Mississippi, hospital. All efforts to save his life had failed, and it was only a matter of days, perhaps hours, until he succumbed. During a visit to the man's bedside, a doctor asked if there were any relatives that needed to be notified. The soldier, too weak to speak, shook his head then reached under the sheets and, with difficulty, withdrew a diary that he handed to the physician. The doctor placed the small, worn journal in his pocket, visited with the patient for a few more minutes, then left to continue his rounds.

That evening, the ex-soldier died. He was buried the following day in a pauper's grave with no one in attendance save for a minister, one city official, and two gravediggers.

A week passed before the doctor had an opportunity to examine the dead soldier's diary. What he read stunned him. It provided a detailed account of the St. Albans raid, the preparations leading up to it, and the aftermath. It described the burying of $120,000 worth of gold coins just a few yards off the St. Albans–Montreal road and the placing of a very heavy, flat rock on top of the cache.

According to the dead man, he was one of the three Rebels who escaped from the St. Albans posse in October 1864. Not wishing to report back to the Confederate headquarters in Montreal, he decided to desert and return to his home in Mississippi. Shortly after the fight, he rode into the woods and turned toward the southwest. For days on end he rode, avoiding settlements and travelers. After two weeks his horse gave out and had to be abandoned. On foot, he eventually made his way to the Ohio River somewhere in Indiana. From there, he hitched a series of boat rides to the Mississippi River, where he built a crude raft and floated southward with the current until finally reaching his Greenville, Mississippi, home.

The doctor, with visions of growing rich from recovering the buried coins, began to make plans to travel to Vermont to search for the location. His position with the hospital, however, kept him busy, and he was never able to manage the time. He held on to the diary for years and then, realizing he would never be able to make the journey, passed it along to a friend. The diary went through several more ownerships over the next few decades before landing in the possession of one Hubert Crane in 1908. Crane, a resident of Birmingham, Alabama, was keenly interested in Civil War history, and, having read the diary of the dead Confederate soldier, became obsessed with finding the buried treasure of gold coins. As soon as he could make the appropriate arrangements, Crane traveled to St. Albans, Vermont.

On arriving, Crane checked in to an established and historic hotel in town and began asking questions of some of the old-timers about the 1864 raid on the banks. Only a handful of people who had been alive in 1864 were left in town. Their memories were dim, and their versions of the event conflicted. None were involved in the pursuit of the Rebel bank robbers into Quebec.

Crane read reports of the event in old newspapers and soon realized all the conclusions were the same: Approximately $120,000 worth of gold coins was buried a few yards off the old St. Albans–Montreal road about two miles south of the Canadian border. The exact location could never be determined. There was nothing for Crane to do but go in search of the treasure himself.

There was one major aspect of the search that Crane regarded as vital—he had to find the large, flat rock that was covering the cache in a pine grove, a rock that required four troopers to move into place. Crane convinced himself the task was not going to be a difficult one.

For days, however, Crane searched the sides of the road in a broad region he identified as having potential. He found not one but several pine groves. The area he selected to search was large, and each day he explored a section of it. Try as he might, though, he was never able to locate the flat rock.

One evening during the second week of his stay in St. Albans, Crane was dining at a local restaurant when he was approached by an old man who politely introduced himself and requested permission to sit and chat. He told Crane he had a story to tell about the buried coins.

Crane welcomed the old man, a native of St. Albans, and listened to his tale. The old fellow told Crane that sometime during the year 1868, a stranger arrived in town and checked himself into the same hotel where Crane was currently registered. Like Crane, this newcomer asked many questions of the residents about the stolen gold and other events associated with the 1864 robbery as well as the flight of the Rebel soldiers back into Canada. Otherwise, the stranger remained quiet and withdrawn.

The stranger, who had a very pronounced Southern accent, rented a horse and wagon from the local livery and spent the greater part of each day exploring around the area near the road north of town and just south of the border. Occasionally, travelers along this road reported seeing the stranger digging in a grove of pine trees about two miles south of the boundary line.

One afternoon, a local farmer who had grown suspicious approached the stranger and demanded he explain what he was doing digging in the woods. The stranger offered evasive answers and appeared confused and unsure of where he was and what he was doing. The farmer, believing the newcomer was daft, left him alone thereafter. More time passed, and the stranger eventually left town, carrying only the battered suitcase he arrived with.

According to Crane, the old man who related the story said the stranger revealed that he was one of the three men who escaped from the St. Albans posse and that he had returned to retrieve the buried gold.

Crane asked the old-timer if he would consent to guiding him out to the location that had been searched by the stranger so that the two of them could look around. Crane was convinced that the flat rock overlying the treasure cache had long been covered over with dirt and forest debris. He planned to mark off a promising region into grids and search each one separately, using a length of thin metal rod to jab into the soft ground in an attempt to find the rock. The old man agreed to take him out to the area.

The next morning, Crane leased a horse-drawn carriage, picked up the old man, and drove out to the region in question. On arriving at what Crane believed to be the approximate site of the treasure cache, both men were surprised and stunned to discover that the entire area had been burned over by an extensive forest fire only a few days earlier. Two hundred acres of woods had been destroyed with not a tree left standing.

The pine grove that many believed was the location of the treasure no longer existed, and the old man was unable to identify even its approximate location. Dejected, Crane and the old man returned to St. Albans. The following day, Crane packed up and returned to Alabama.

As far as anyone knows, the trove of $120,000 in 1860s-era gold coins buried by the raiding Confederates has never been found, and to this day many are convinced that it lies only a few inches below the surface somewhere in the second-growth timber north of St. Albans and just a couple of miles from the Canadian border. Men who have researched the tale are convinced that the treasure still lies beneath a large, flat rock and just a few yards to the left or right of the old road and not far from the small community of Highgate Springs.

Today, Interstate 89 has replaced the old St. Albans–Montreal road. Many hopeful treasure hunters have searched both sides of this highway for the treasure cache to no avail. What they apparently did not know is that the interstate does not precisely follow the old road, which lies dozens of yards to one side. From the air, however, the old road through the woods is still apparent.

The cache, if located today, is estimated by coin collectors to be worth in the tens of millions of dollars in real and antique value.

INDEX

A

American Civil War. *See* Civil
    War

Ames, Sgt. James F., 115, 117

Appalachian Mountains, gold in,
    95–96

Arkansas
    Callahan Mountain treasure,
        51–52
    weapons in Cross Hollows,
        48–50

B

Battle for Fort Macon, 125–26,
    127–28

Battle of Parker's Crossroads, 32,
    33

Battle of the Wilderness, 100

Bechtler, August, 86, 88

Bechtler, Christopher, 85–86, 87

Bechtler, Christopher (Junior),
    86, 88

Black, P. H., 92–93

blue quartz. *See* quartz, gold-filled

Boucher, Dr., 55, 56

Bragg, Gen., 71, 73

Breckenridge, John C., 66

Brooks, Corp. Allen E., 112

Brushy Creek Valley. *See* Fletcher,
    Corp. Henry

Buckhannon River Valley (WV),
    118, 121, 122

Burlington (NC), 93

Burnside, Gen. Amborse, 126,
    127, 128

C

Callahan Mountain (AR), 51–52

Casteel, Ben, 79

Chambliss, Allen, 32, 34–35

Chapmanville (WV), 124

Chatata (TN), 76–77, 78–79

Chennault, Rev. Dionysius, 68,
    69

Cherokee Indians, Chatata
    community of, 76

Civil War, 141
    battle at Callahan Mountain,
        51–52
    battle at Prairie Grove, 40–43
    Battle for Fort Macon, 125–26,
        127–28
    Battle of the Wilderness, 100
    in Coffee County, 36

Confederate Army silver,
134–40
England's support for
Confederacy, 22–23
in Fayette County (WV), 123
Indian Territory in, 58
in Madison County, 26
Parker's Crossroads battle, 32,
33
soldiers' payroll chest, 31–35
wealth hidden or lost during,
vii, x
weapons at Cross Hollows,
48–50
See also Confederate States
of America; Union Army;
specific states
Clark, Capt. Micajah, 67
Cobb County (GA), coin cache
in, 5–10
Coffee County (TN), 36
Cohutta Mountain (GA), gold at,
96–99
Confederate Army of Tennessee,
attack on train, 77–78
Confederate States of America,
141
and Bechtler coins, 86
payrolls of, 40–43, 134–40
and Rutherfordton mint, 84
support in Canada for, 142
treasury of, 62–69, 90–94
See also Civil War
Crane, Hubert, 145–46, 147
Crismo, John, 106–9

Cross Hollows (AR), weapons at,
48–50
Cunningham, Peter, 38
Curtis, Maj. Gen. Samuel R., 48,
49
Custer, Gen. George Armstrong,
117
Cynthiana (KY), raid on, 74, 75

D
Davis, Mrs. Varina, 63, 64
Davis, Pres. Jefferson, 62, 64,
65–66, 67
Denman, H. L., 9
Dobbs, Mr., 136–40
Duchase, Capt. J. W., 90–92
Duke, Gen. Basil, 66, 67–68
Dunham, Col. C. L., 31–34, 35

E
Enfield rifles. *See Minho* (ship)
England, support for Confederacy,
22–24

F
Fayette County (WV), 123
Fletcher, Corp. Henry, 1–4
Fletcher, Mr., 99
Flowers, Mr., 13, 15
Forrest, Nathan Bedford, 31, 32,
33, 35
Fort Macon. *See* Battle for Fort
Macon
Frasier, Trenholm, and Co. *See*
Minho (ship)

Frisby, Col. Norman, 11–16
Fuller, Artie, 26–30
Fuller, Jessie, 27, 29, 30

G
Georgia
   coin cache in Cobb County,
     5–10
   Lipscomb's plantation in,
     44–47
   Sherman's march in, 7
gold
   Bechtler's coins, 86–89
   cache in Cobb County, 5–10
   in Cohutta Mtn., 96–99
   Confederate States of
     America's, 40–43, 62–69, 75,
     90–94
   Crismo's, 107–9
   Frisby's buried fortune, 14–16
   Fuller's, 26–27, 29, 30
   Hall's cache, 53, 54, 56–57
   Henderson County cave,
     100–105
   Lipscomb's, 44–47
   Morgan's, 70–71, 75
   Mosby's, 115–17
   in North Carolina, 84–85
   Parlange's, 18–21
   in quartz, 2–4, 95–96
   Smith's, 110, 112–13
   in Tasso (TN), 76, 78, 79–80
   Union Army payrolls, 123–24
   Usray's, 59–61
   Wenten's, 37–39

   in *York Castle*, 23, 25
   *See also specific individuals,
     locations*
Gore, Sgt., 126–27, 128–29
Grant, Gen. Ulysses S., 31, 62
Gray Ghost. *See* Mosby, Gen.
   John Singleton
Grierson, James, 107
Griffith, Pvt. Isaac, 77

H
Hadley, Lt. J. H., 100–105
Hall, Alonzus, 53–57
Harmon's Cave, 113
   See also Poor Valley (VA)
Harrington, Sgt. Jack, 112
Hassler, William, 96–97
Henderson County (NC), cave in,
   100–105
Hurst, Fielding, 27, 28–29

J
Johnson, Titus, 47

L
Lafitte, Jean, 12
Laurel Caverns (PA), 136, 139
Lee, Gen. Robert E., 62
Lipscomb, Mr., plantation of,
   44–47

M
Maynard, John, 8–9
McCulloch, Gen. Ben, 48, 49
McCullough, W. F., 54, 55, 56

McWhorter, Lucullus Virgil, 120, 121

Minho (ship), 130–33

Morgan, Gen. John H., 70–75

Mosby, Gen. John Singleton, 114, 115–17

Mount Sterling (KY), raid on, 74

Mullins, James, 98–99

N

Ninth Michigan Cavalry, attack by, 73

North Carolina
Battle for Fort Macon, 125–28
gold in, 84–85, 86
Henderson County cave, 100–105

O

Ouachita Mountains, 3, 4

P

Parker, Capt. William H., 62–65, 67

Parlange, Charles, 17, 18, 19–20

Parlange, Virginie, 17–20

Parlange, Walter, 17

Pence (soldier), 97–98

Pender, Capt. Josiah, 125

Poindexter, Pvt. Joseph, 126–27, 128

Poor Valley (VA), 110–11, 113

Prairie Grove (AR), battle at, 40–43

Q

quartz, gold-filled
in Appalachian Mountains, 95, 96
Fletcher's find, 1–4

R

Reagan, John H., 66

Rogersville (TN), silver coins at, 81–83

Rutherfordton (NC)
and Bechtler coins, 86–89
mint at, 84

S

Sellers, Jim, 98–99

silver
in Buckhannon River Valley, 118–22
Confederate States of America's, 62–69, 75, 134–40
Frisby's, 12–16
Morgan's, 71, 75
Parlange's, 18–21
in Tasso (TN), 76, 78, 79, 80
Union Army's, 81–83
Wenten's, 38, 39
See also specific individuals, locations

Sledge (slave), 44, 45, 46

Smith, Abraham, 110, 112

Smith, Eli, 110, 111, 112

Smith, Samuel, 110, 112, 113

Smithsonian Institution, and Bechtler coins, 87

St. Albans (VT), robbery at, 142–48

Stoneman, Gen. George, 63, 110

Stoughton, Edwin H., 114–15, 117

Stuart, Gen. J. E. B., 114, 117

Sugar Grove (Arkansas), 1

Swift, Jonathan, 122

T

Tasso, Mr., 79

Tasso (TN), 76

   gold in, 79–80

Ternant, Marquis Vincent de, 19

Thirty-Ninth Iowa Division, 32

Trent Affair, 22

   See also York Castle (warship)

U

Union Army, payroll shipments of, 31–35, 81–83, 123–24

Usray (Cherokee), 58–61

V

Venable, Bobby, 82, 83

Vermont, gold robbery in, 141

W

weapons caches, x

   at Cross Hollows, 48–50

   in the *Minho,* 130–33

Wells (soldier), 97, 98

Wenten, Cephus, 36–37, 39

West Virginia. *See* Buckhannon River Valley (WV); Fayette Co. (WV)

Wigg, George, 131

Wilson, Joseph A., 119–21

Wilson, Mr., 118, 119

Y

York Castle (warship), 23–25

Young, Capt. Bennett H., 137, 142, 143, 144

ABOUT THE AUTHOR

W. C. Jameson is the award-winning author of over one hundred books and more than 1,500 published articles and essays. A professional treasure hunter for five decades, he has led or participated in over two hundred expeditions in the United States and Mexico. He served as an adviser to the movie *National Treasure* and has appeared on the Discovery Channel, the History Channel, the Travel Channel, National Public Radio, and *Nightline*. He lives in Llano, Texas.